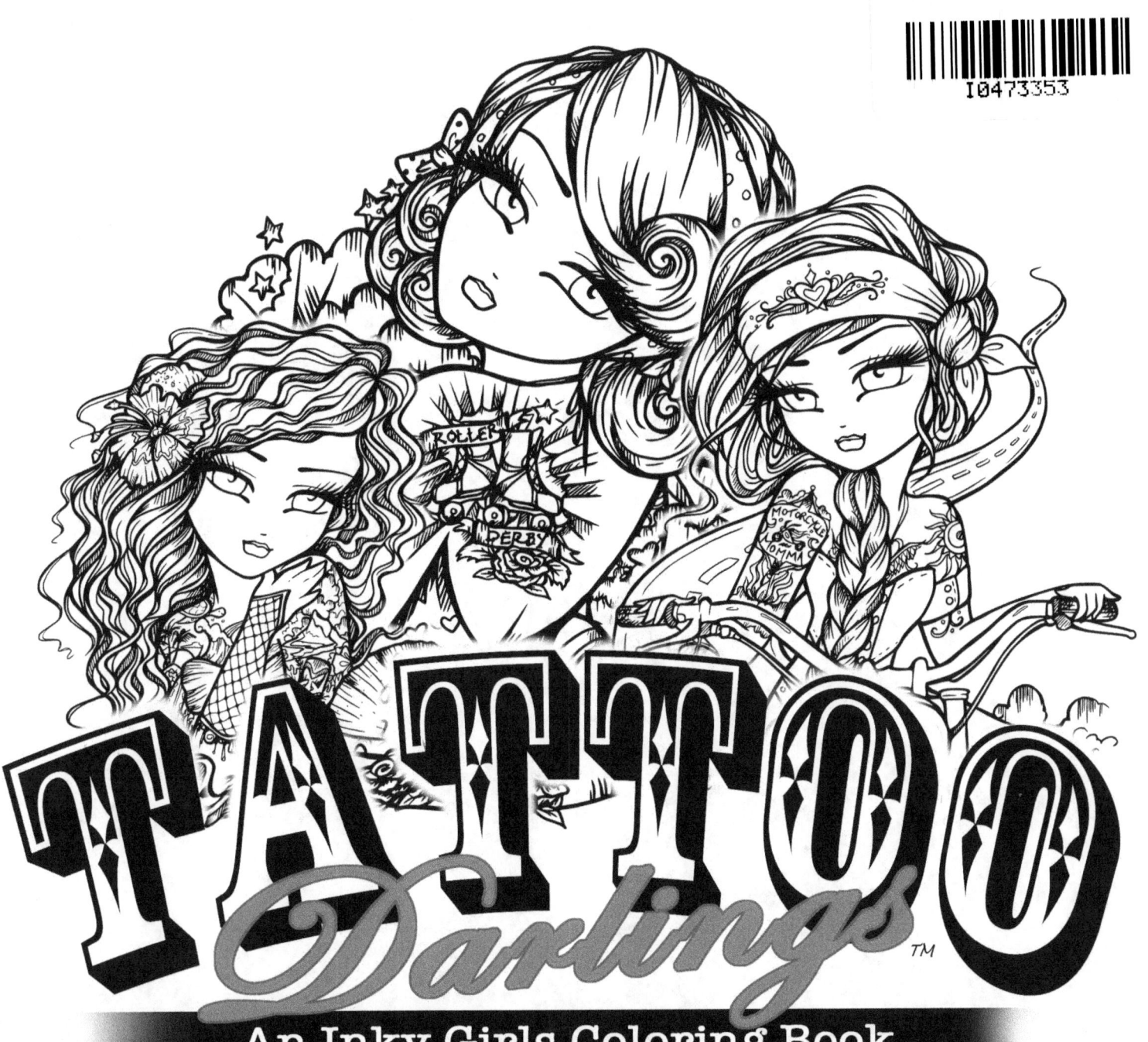

TATTOO *Darlings*™

An Inky Girls Coloring Book

Illustrated by Hannah Lynn

www.HannahLynn.com

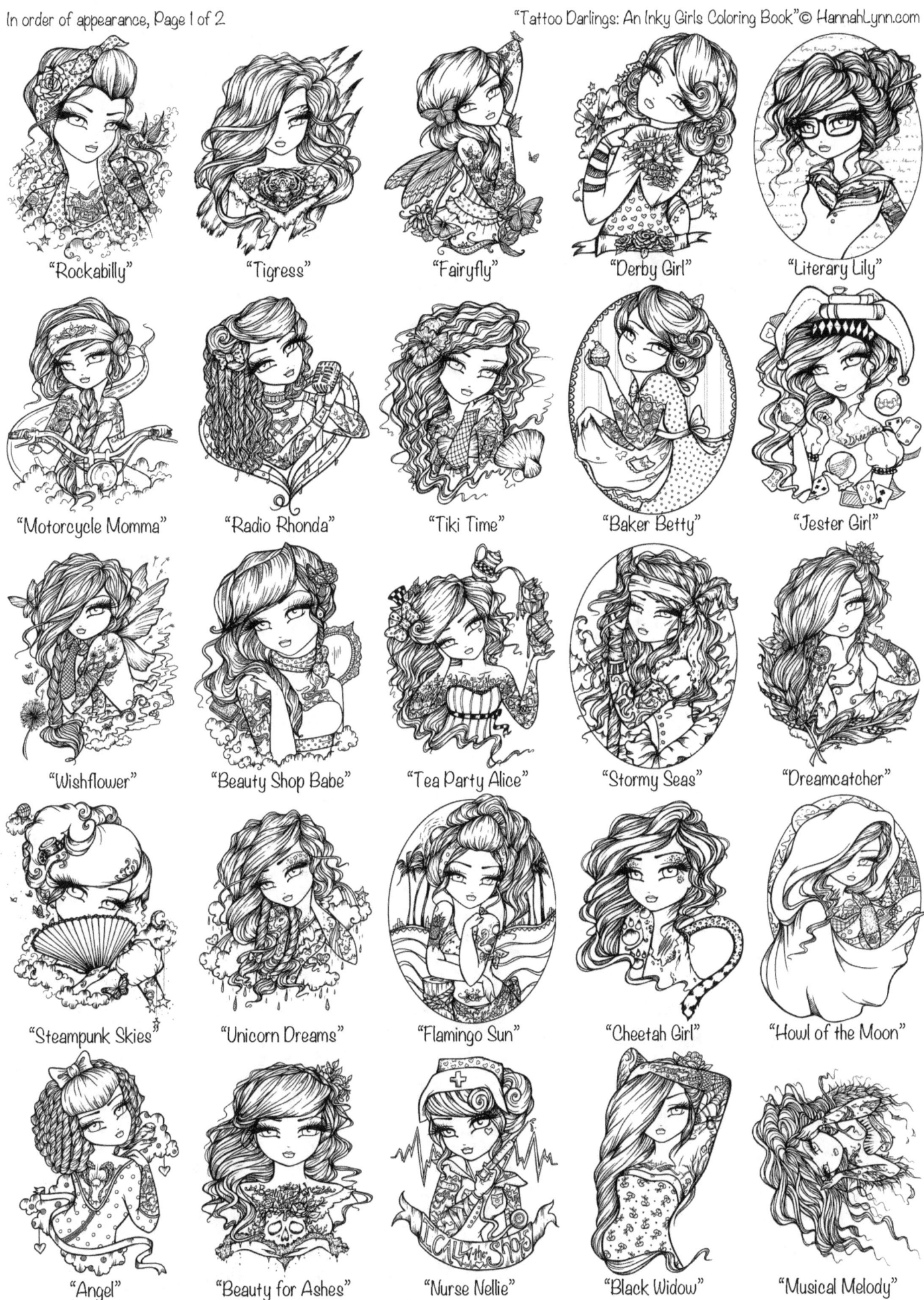

"Rockabilly" "Tigress" "Fairyfly" "Derby Girl" "Literary Lily"

"Motorcycle Momma" "Radio Rhonda" "Tiki Time" "Baker Betty" "Jester Girl"

"Wishflower" "Beauty Shop Babe" "Tea Party Alice" "Stormy Seas" "Dreamcatcher"

"Steampunk Skies" "Unicorn Dreams" "Flamingo Sun" "Cheetah Girl" "Howl of the Moon"

"Angel" "Beauty for Ashes" "Nurse Nellie" "Black Widow" "Musical Melody"

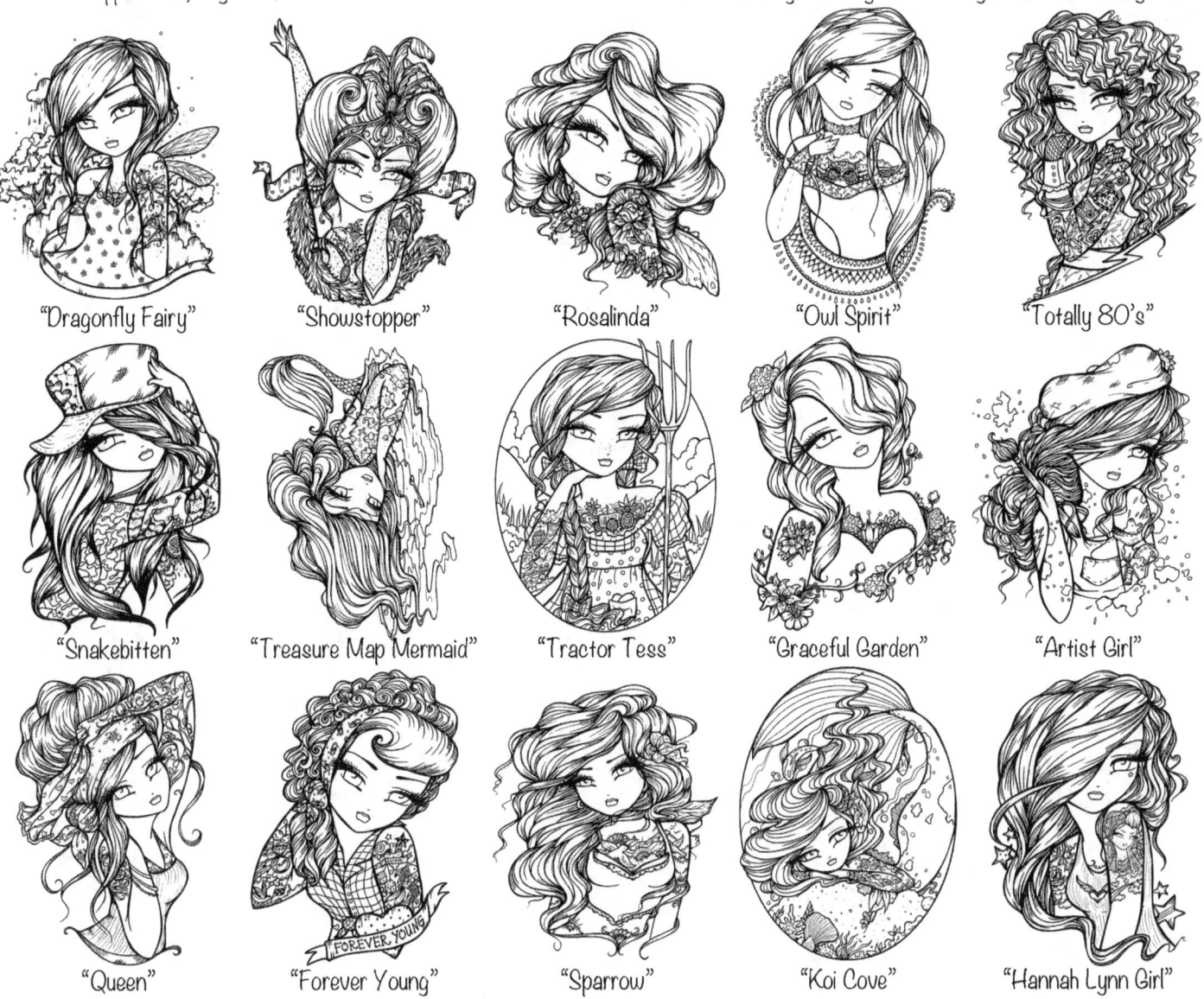

"Dragonfly Fairy"   "Showstopper"   "Rosalinda"   "Owl Spirit"   "Totally 80's"

"Snakebitten"   "Treasure Map Mermaid"   "Tractor Tess"   "Graceful Garden"   "Artist Girl"

"Queen"   "Forever Young"   "Sparrow"   "Koi Cove"   "Hannah Lynn Girl"

A few things before you begin...Place a small stack of copy paper (4-5 sheets) behind the page you are coloring on to eliminate bleed-through and indentation marks to other pages in your book. Please note that really wet mediums aren't recommended on this paper (I do offer PDF printable versions for those that prefer to print on their own paper on HannahLynn.com).

There are no rules with art! The grass doesn't have to be green, and tree trunks don't have to be brown. Don't be afraid to use a mixture of different materials. Have fun with it, and if you feel that you have made a "mistake", don't fret! Every artist, including myself, experiences a period of uncertainty during each piece. Art is fluid. If you keep going, you will see that it works out in the end and gain more confidence from seeing it through! If you feel like you need a break, come back to it with fresh eyes later.

The best way to improve your skills is through experience. So get your materials out, turn on some music that inspires you, and HAVE FUN!!!

For more books, art, & freebies please visit my website at HannahLynn.com!

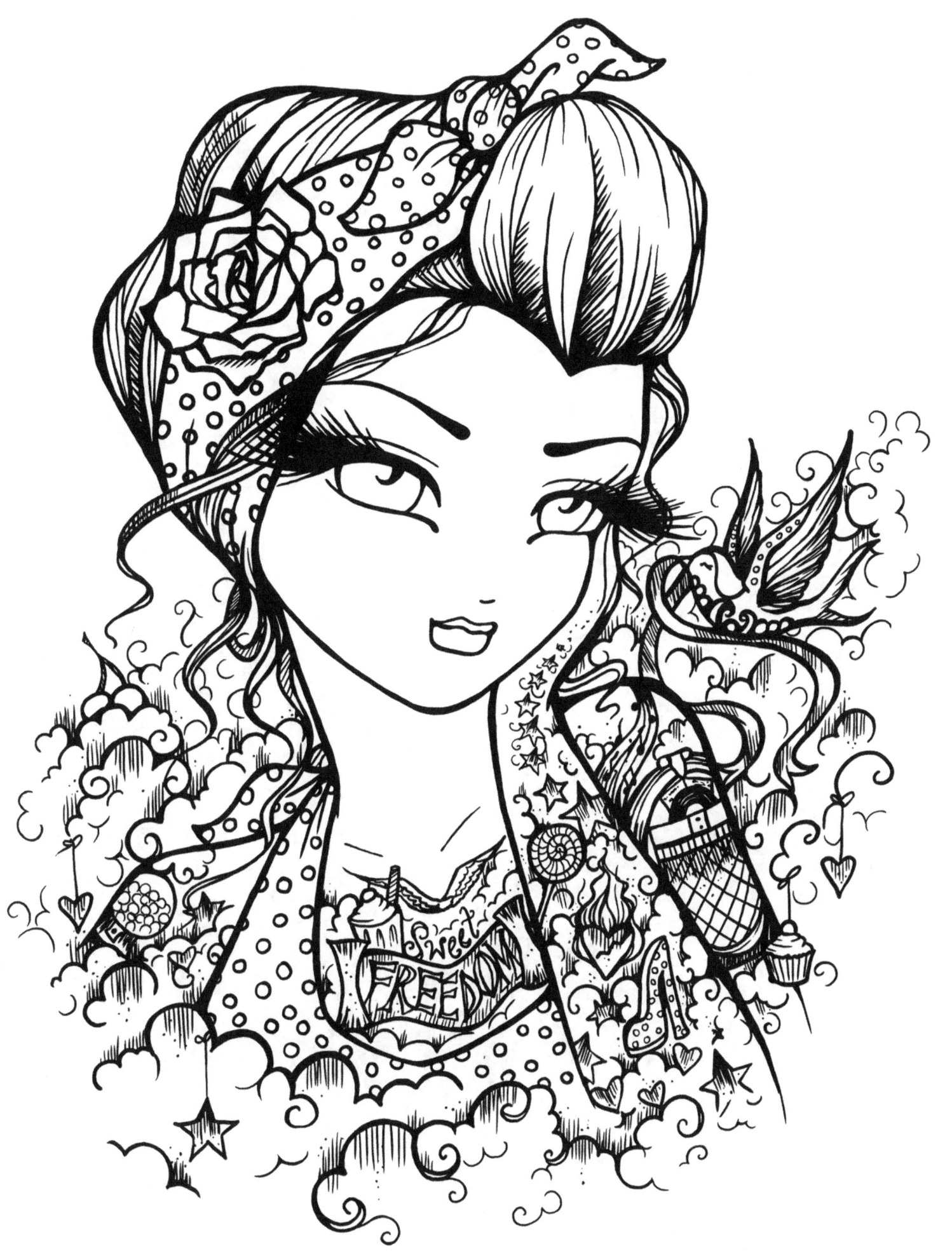

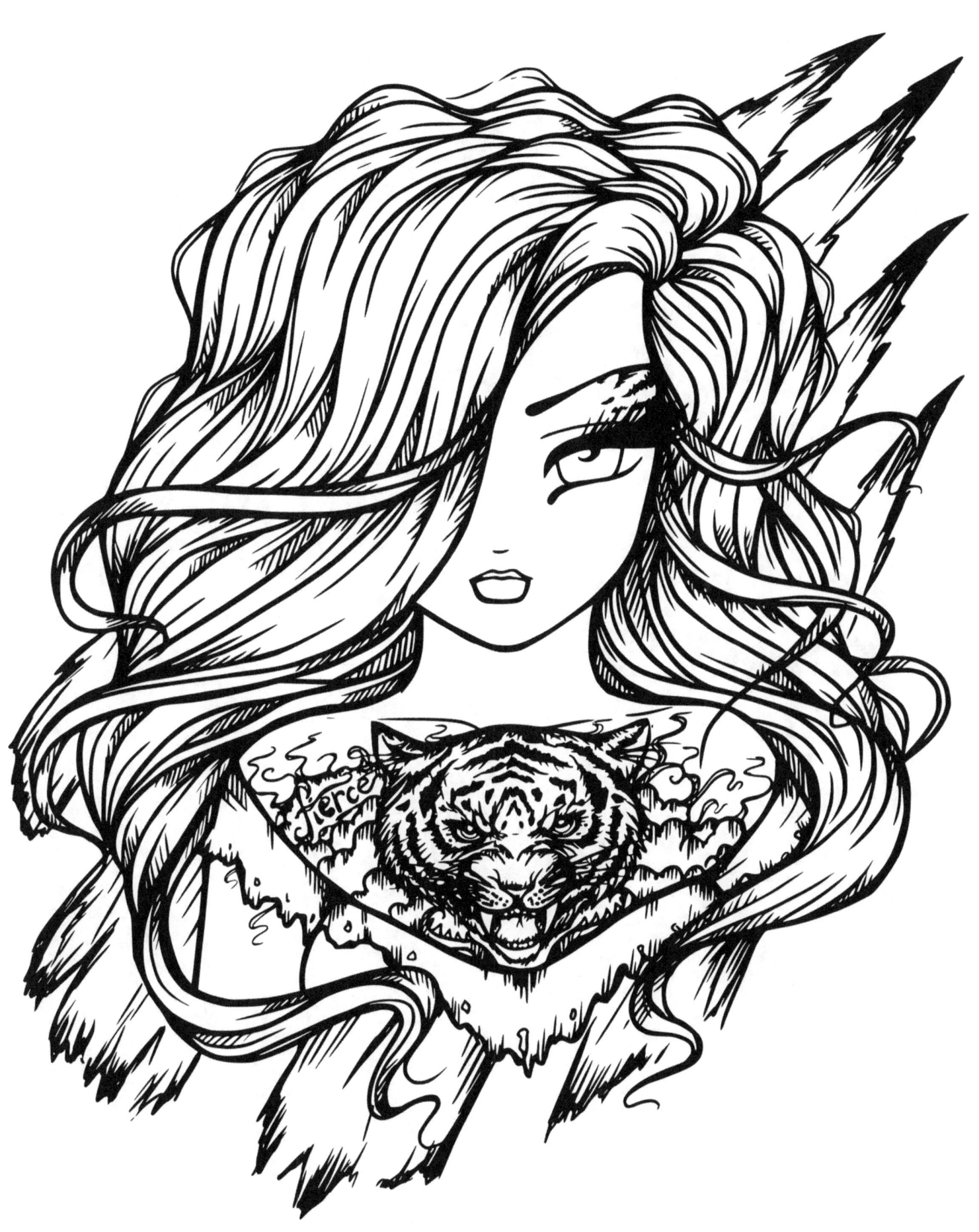

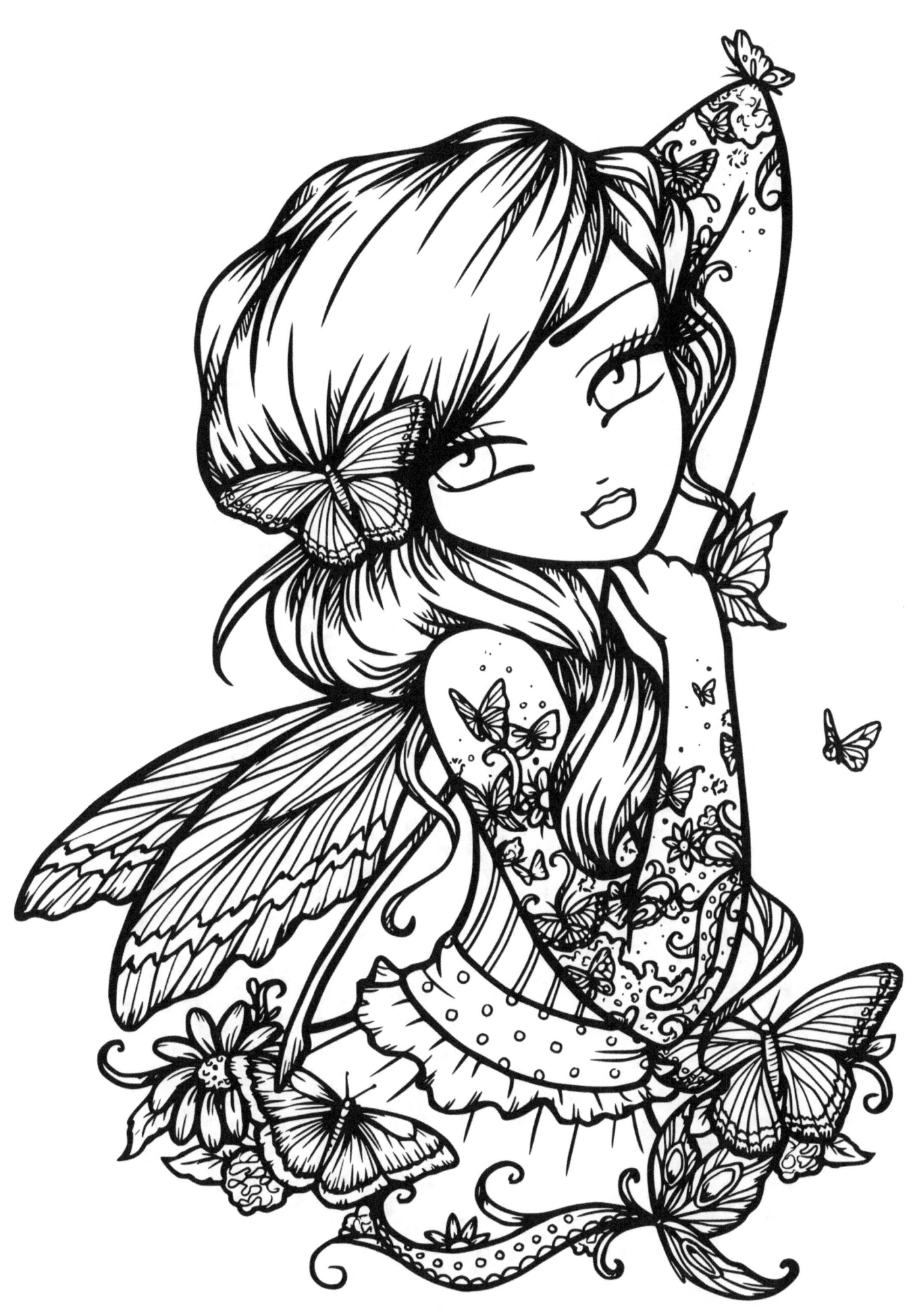

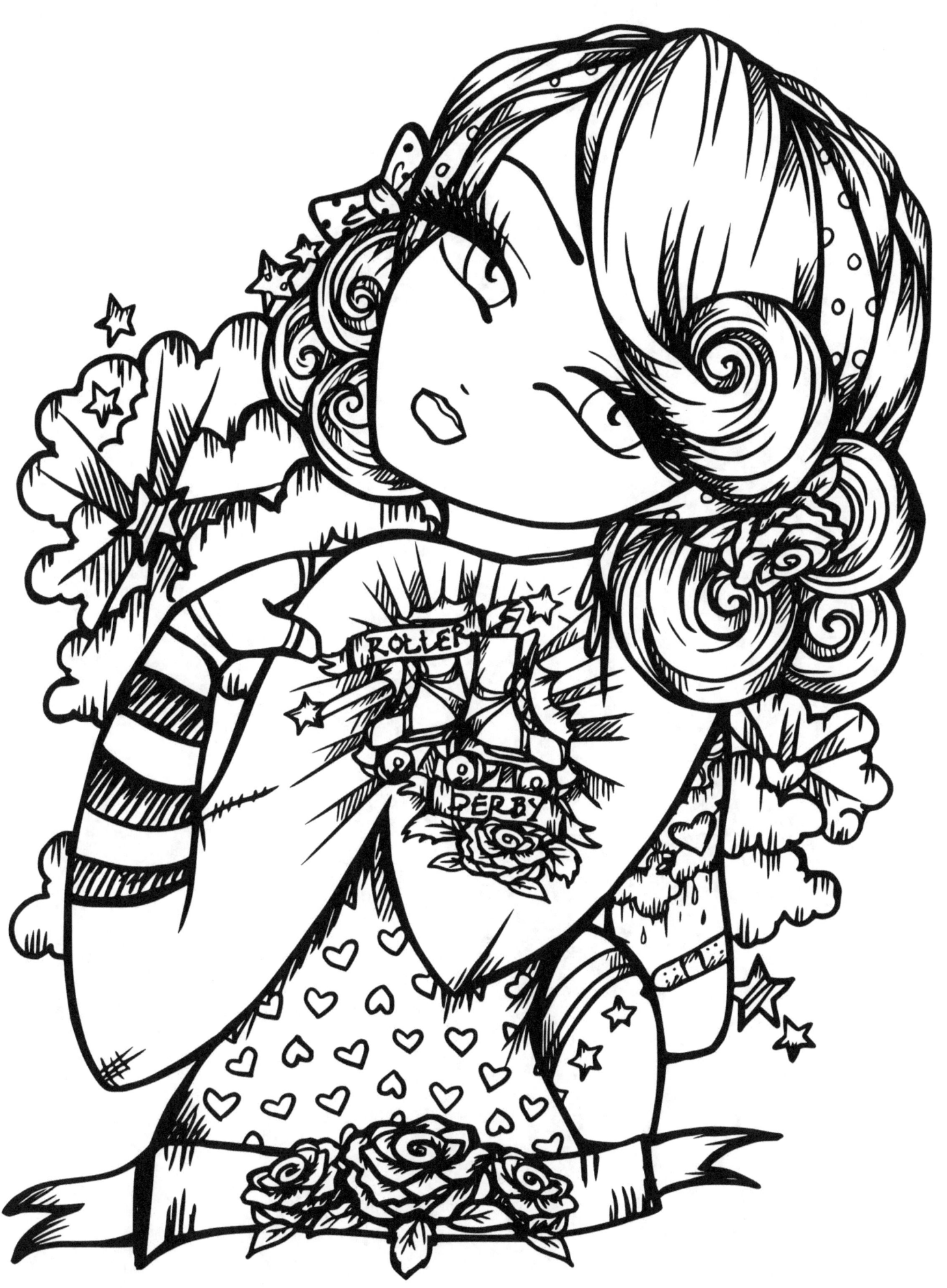

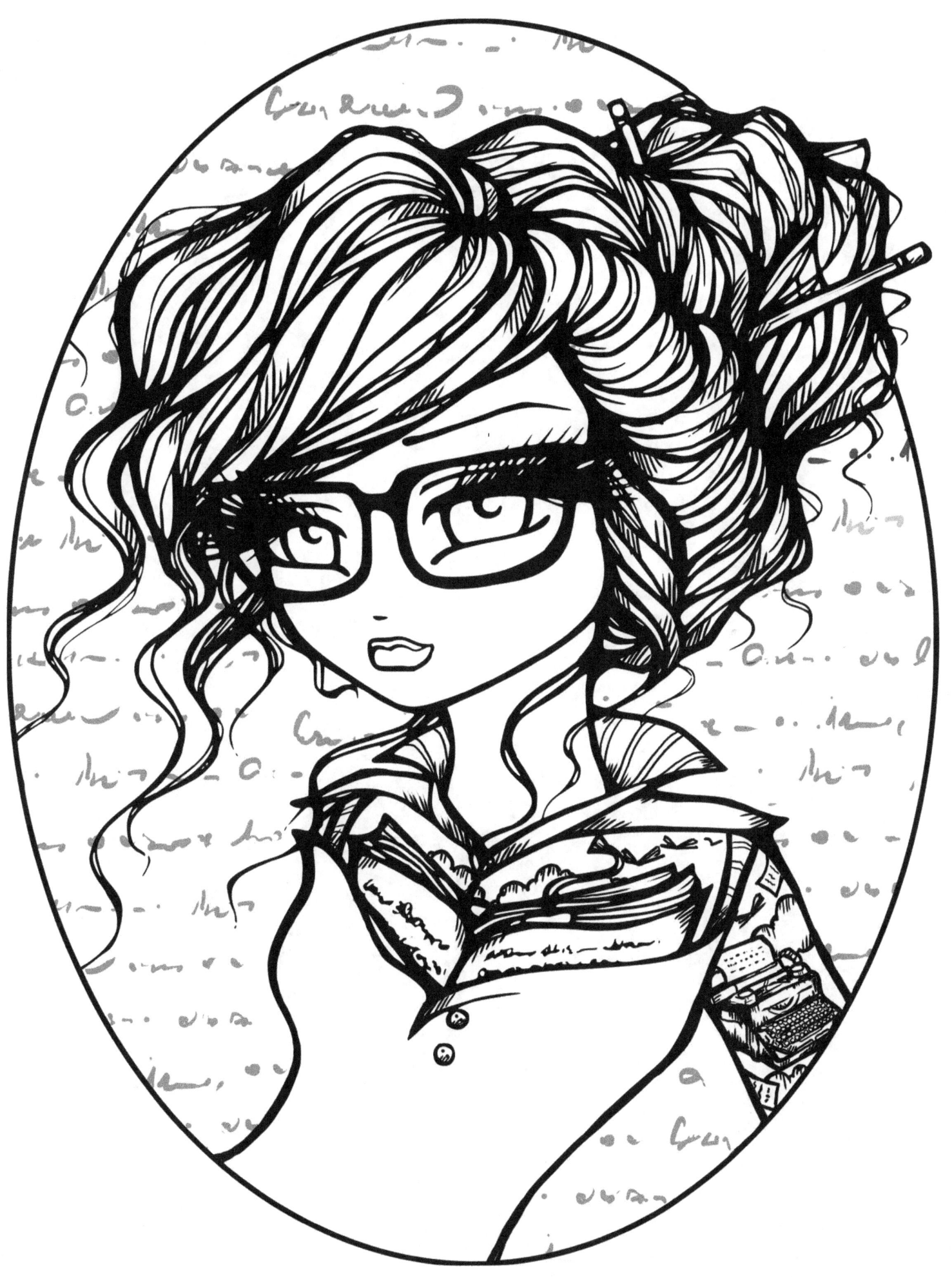

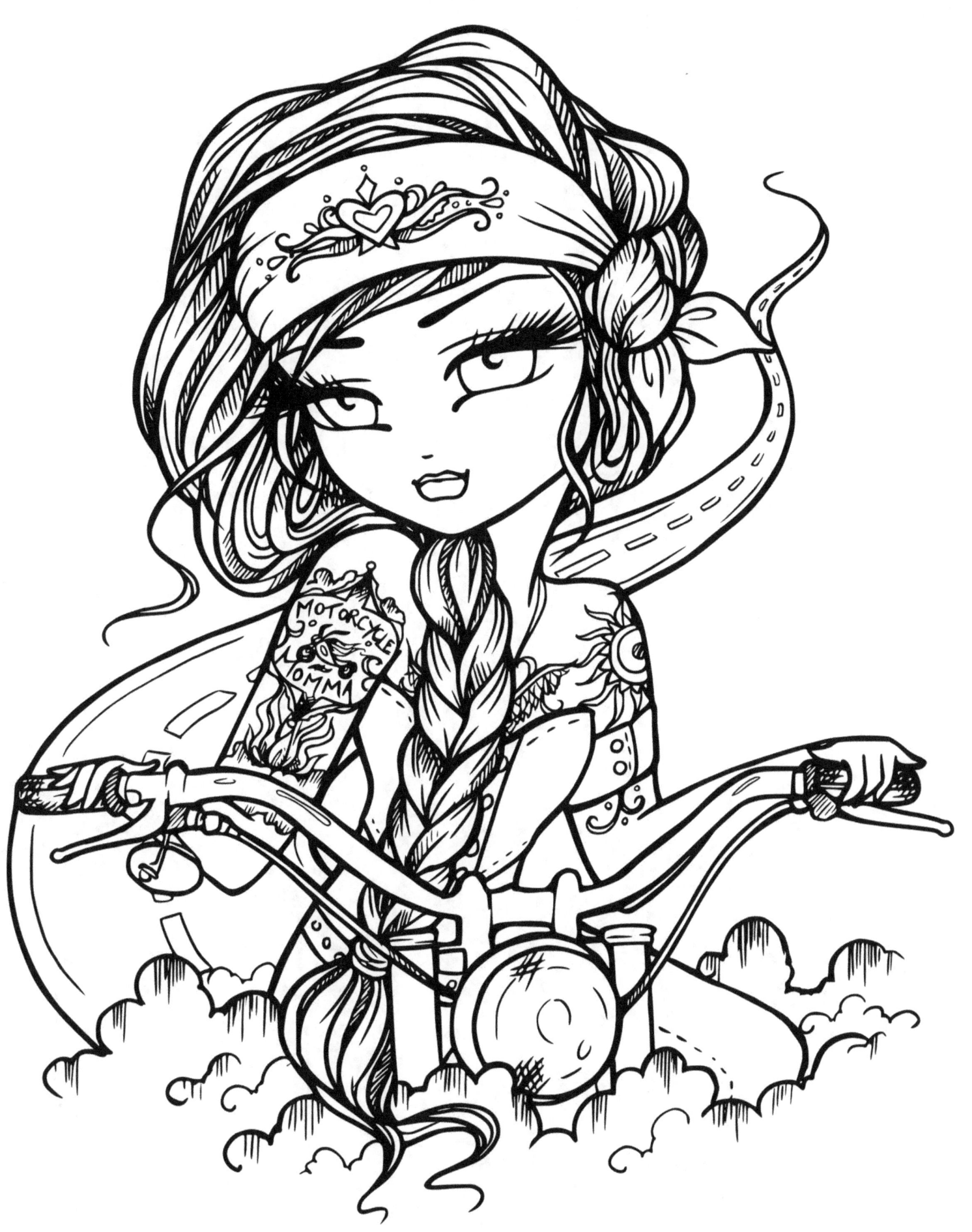

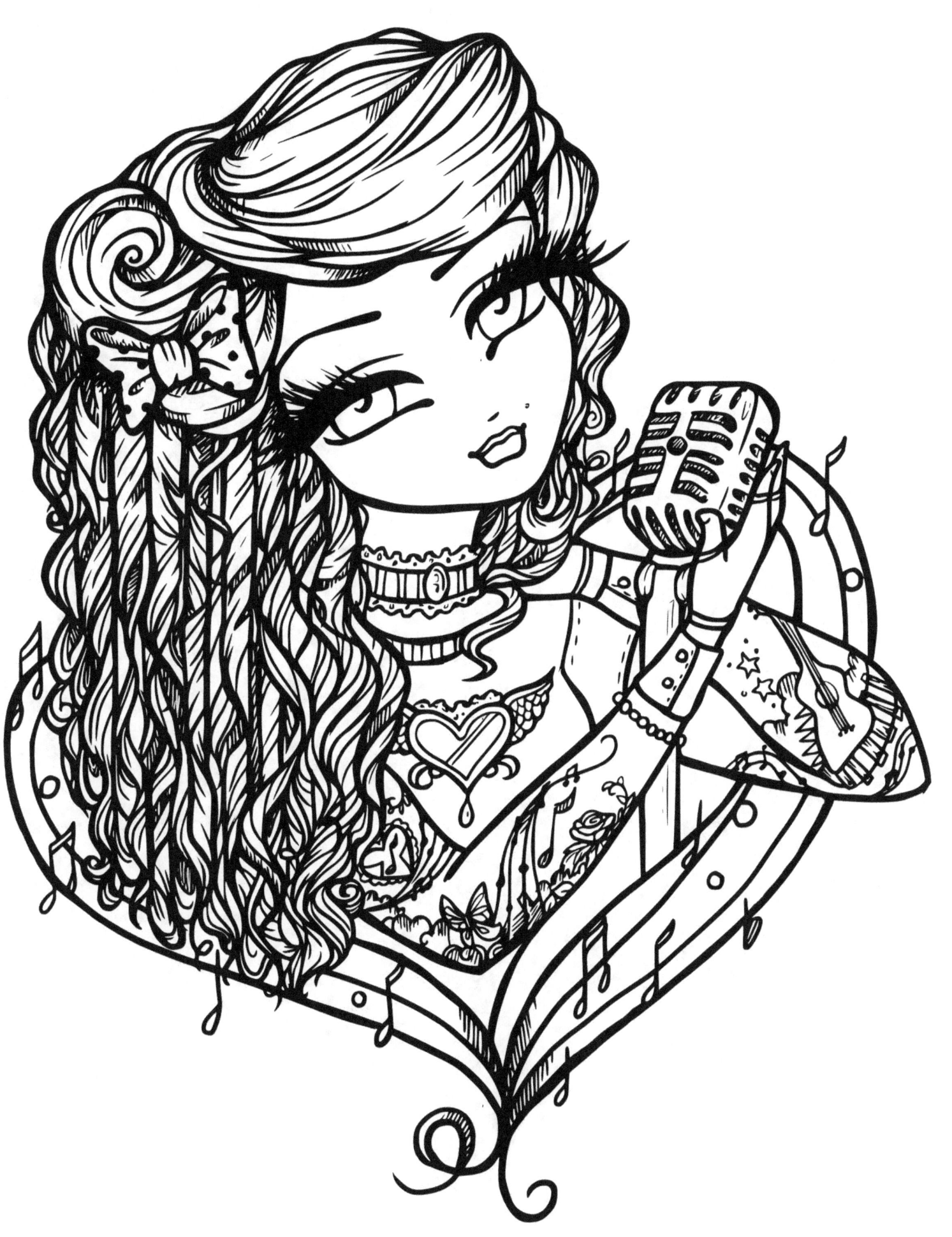

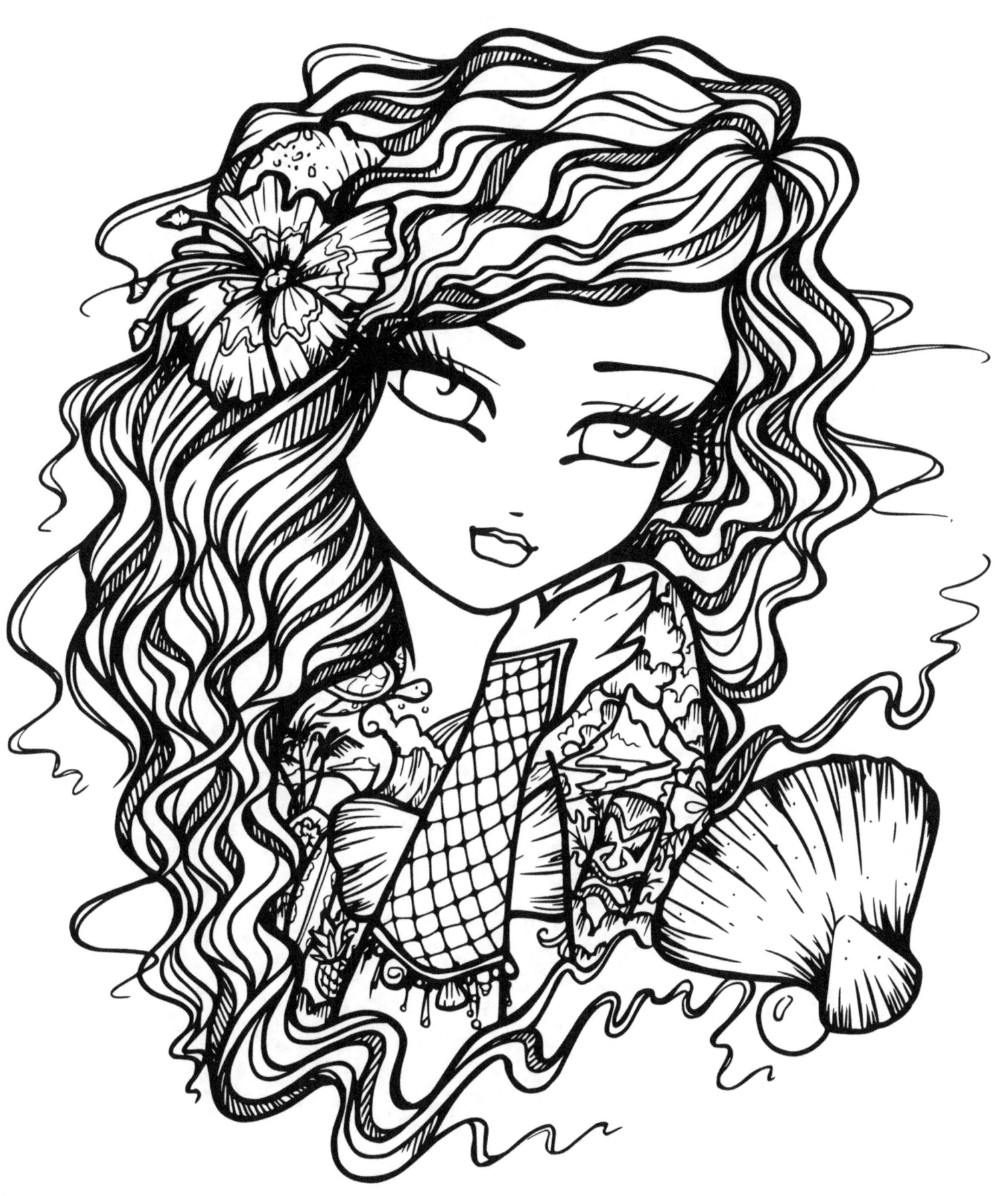

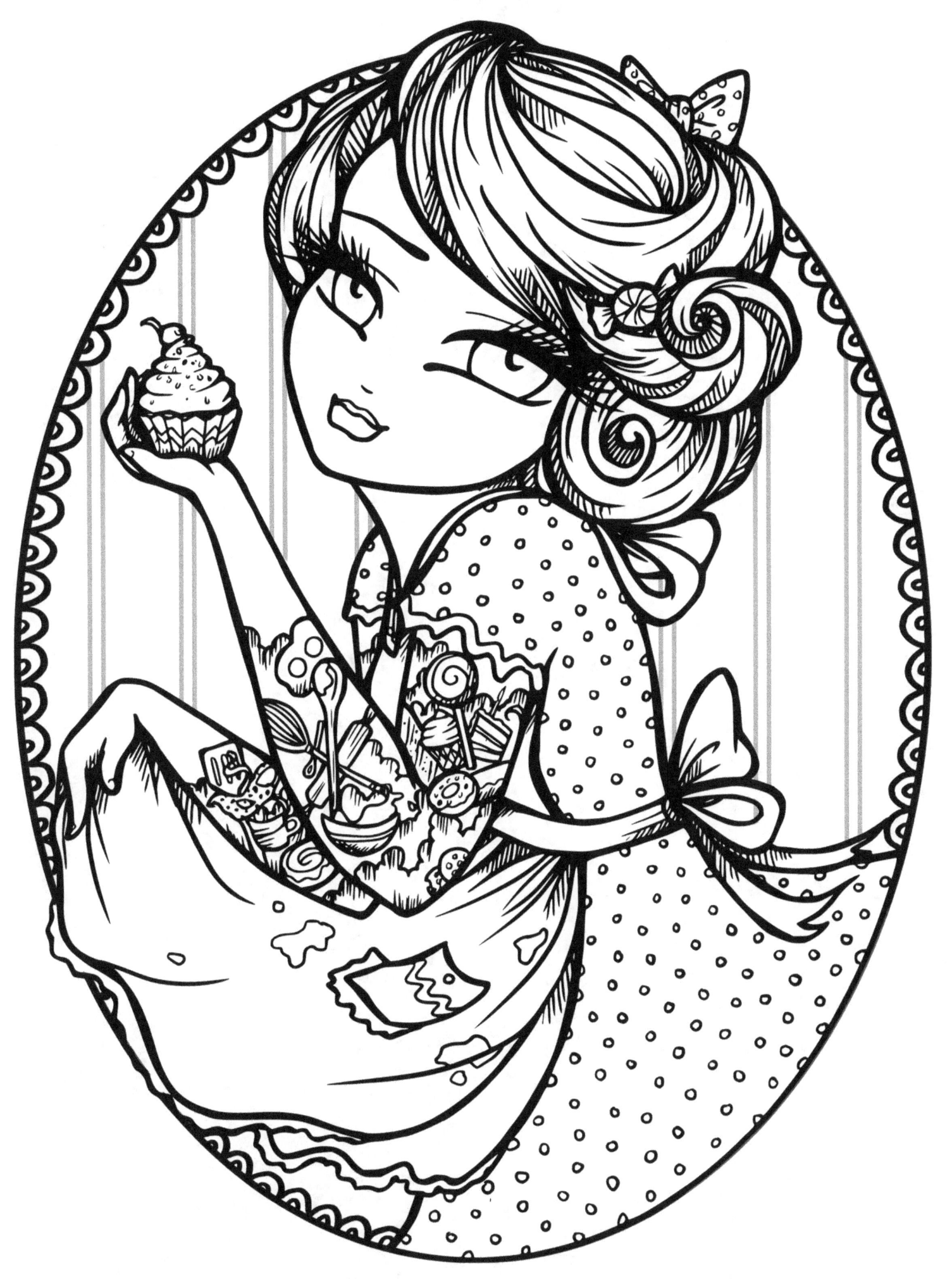

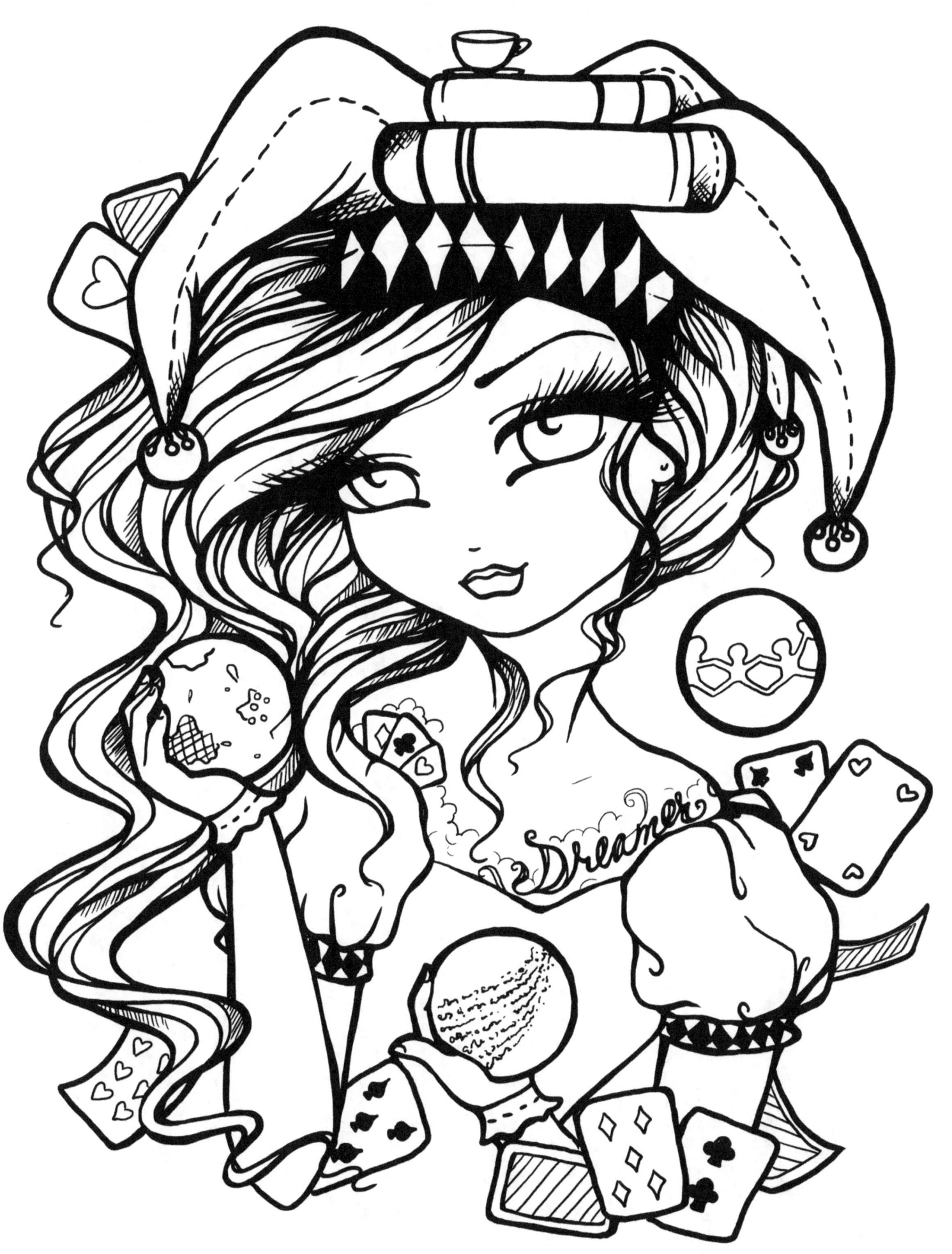

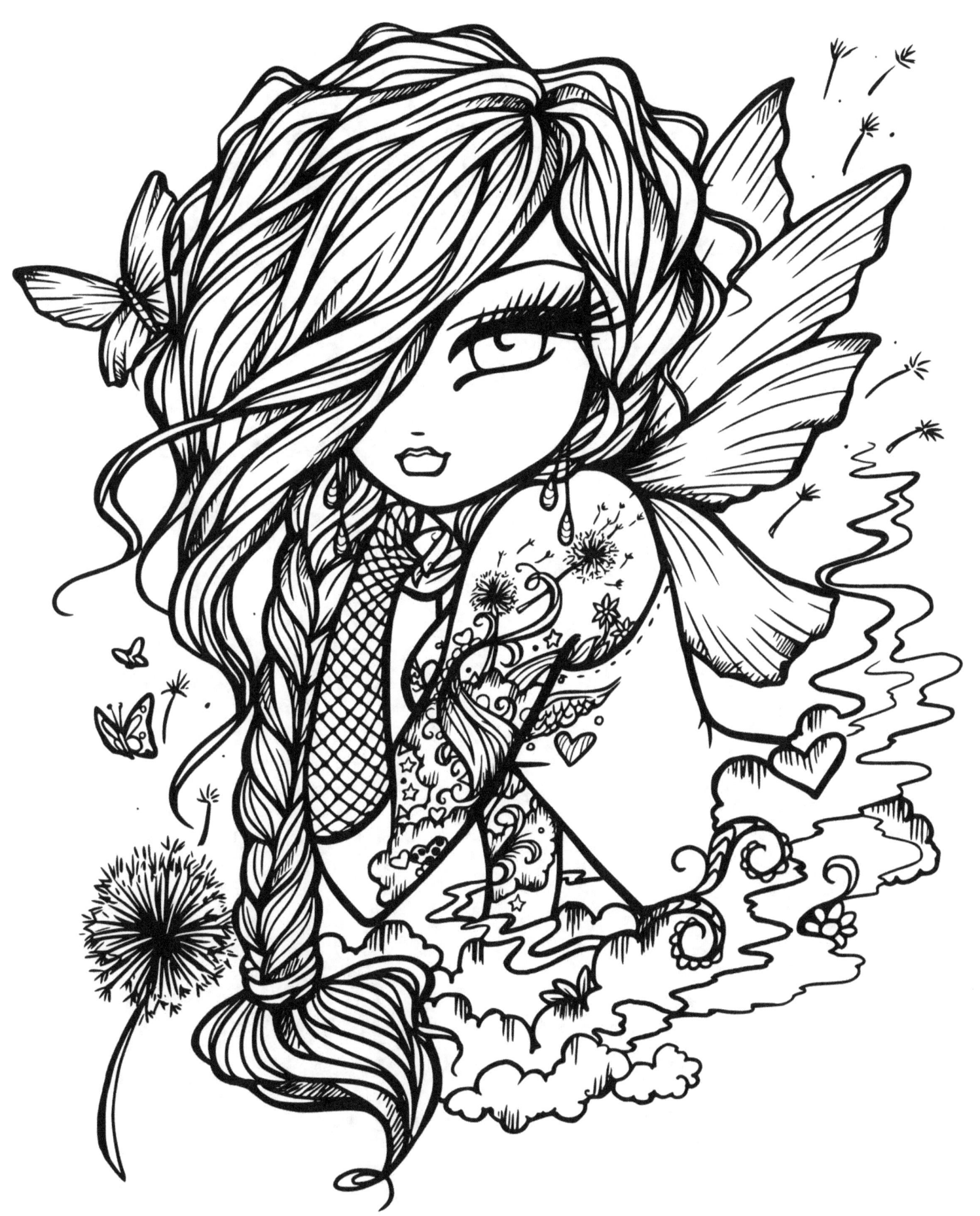

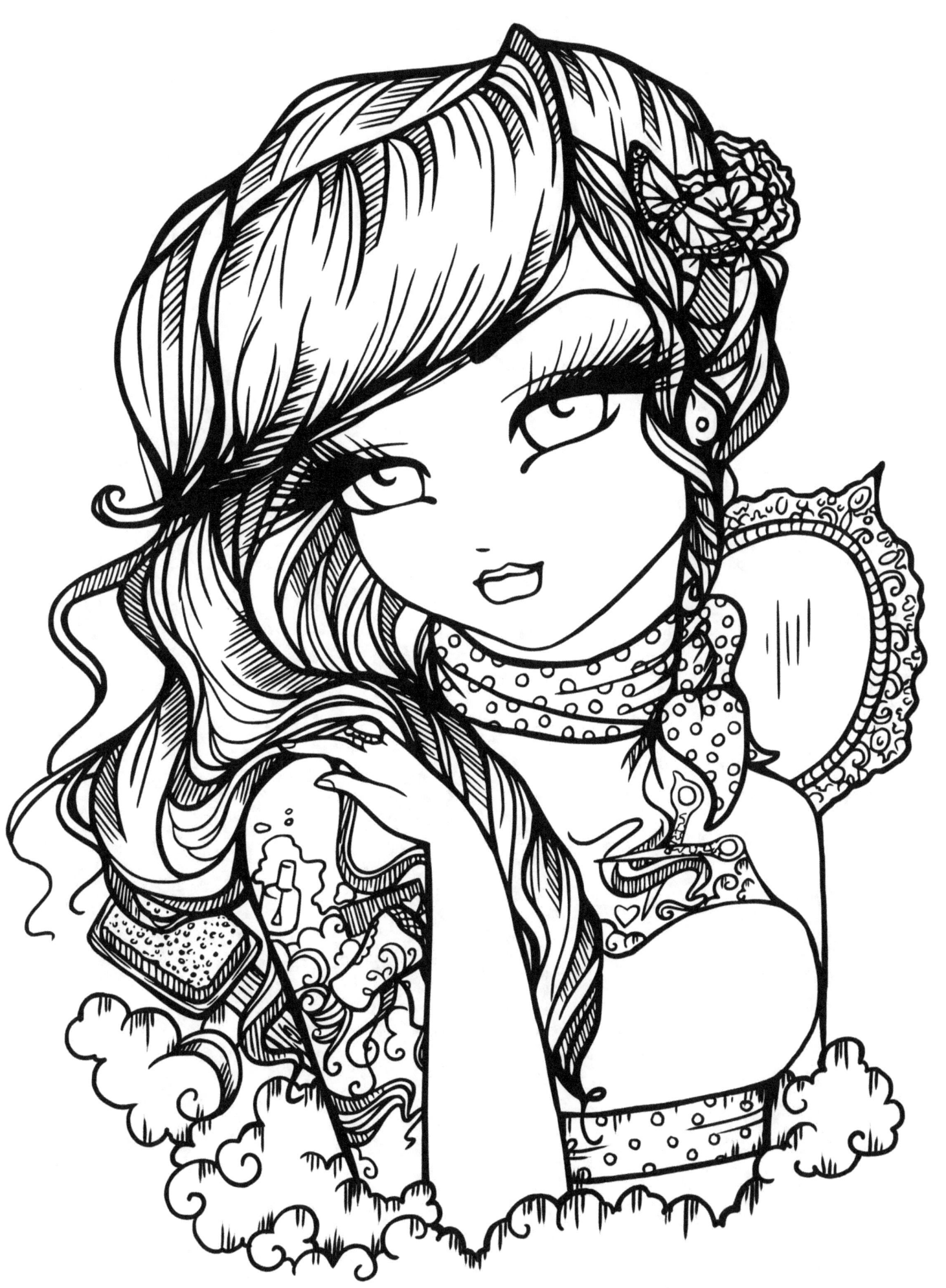

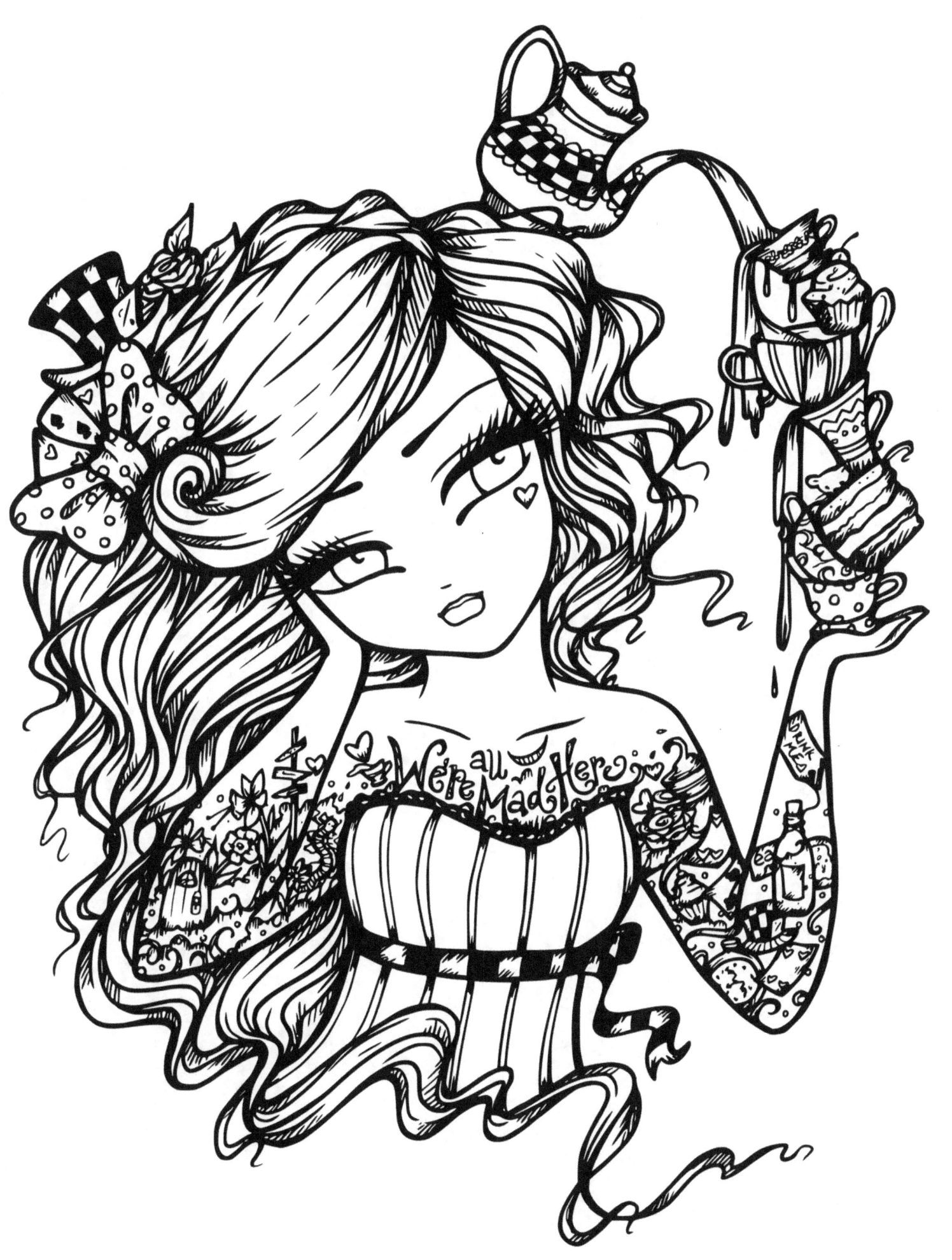

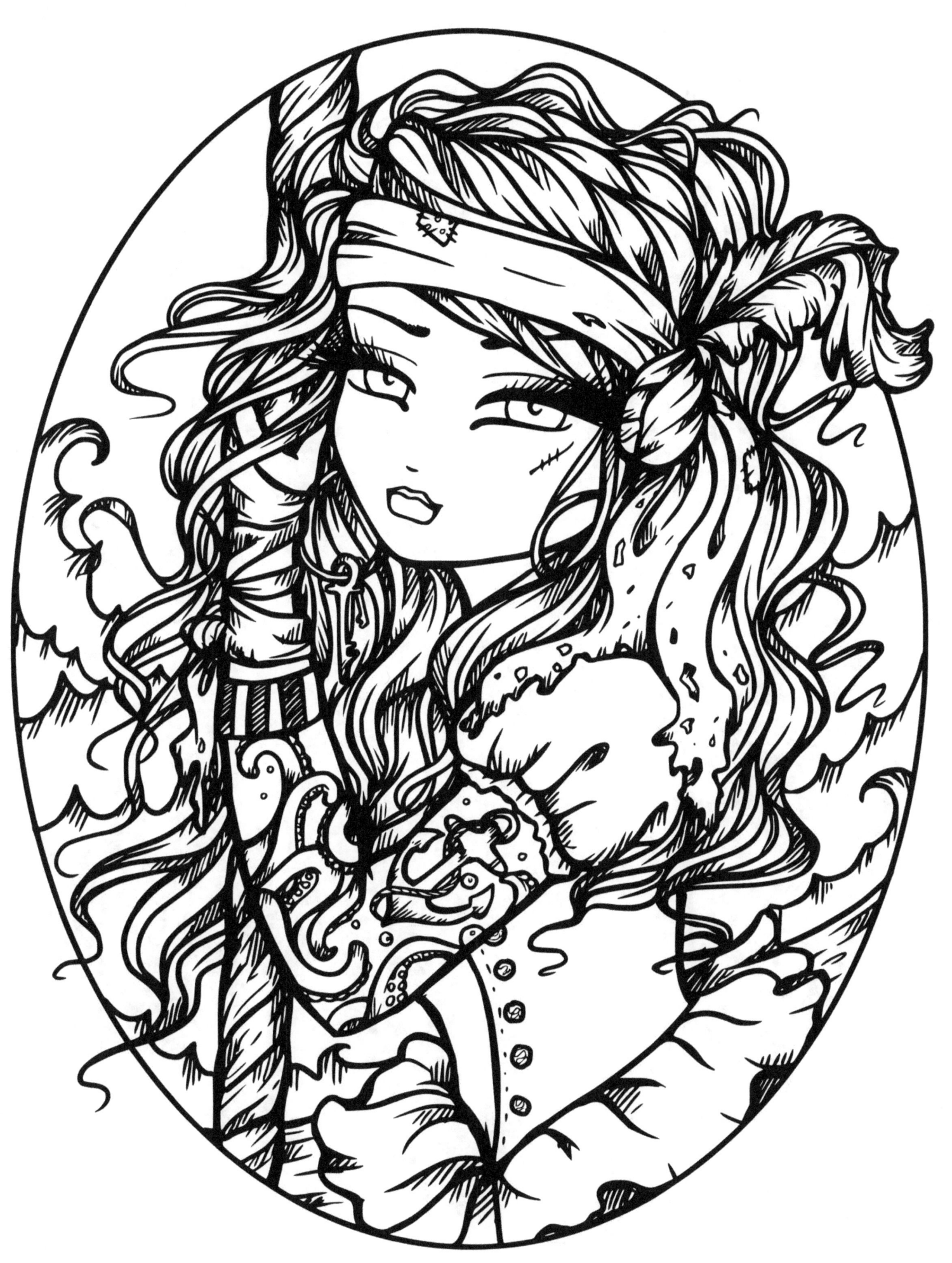

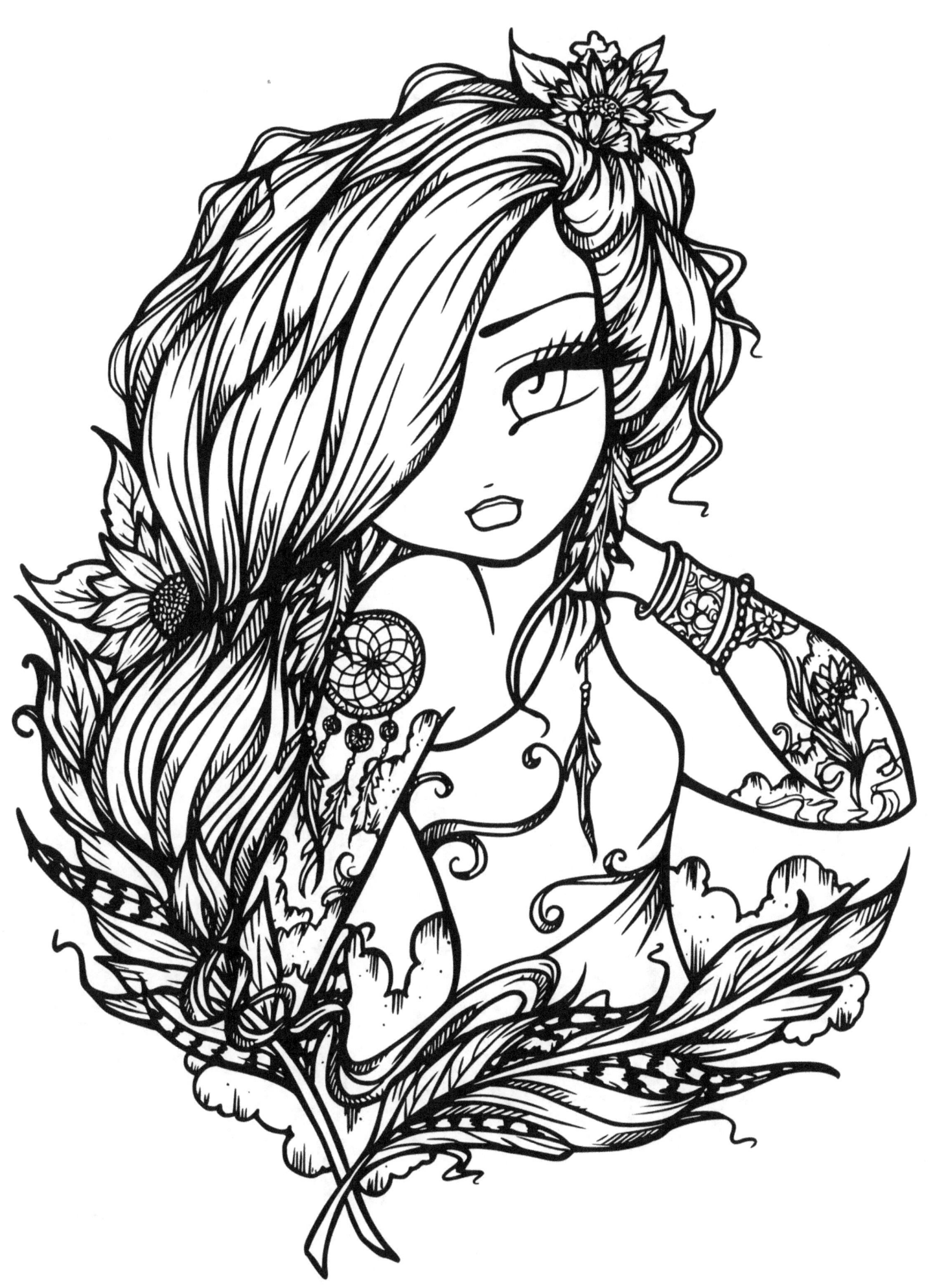

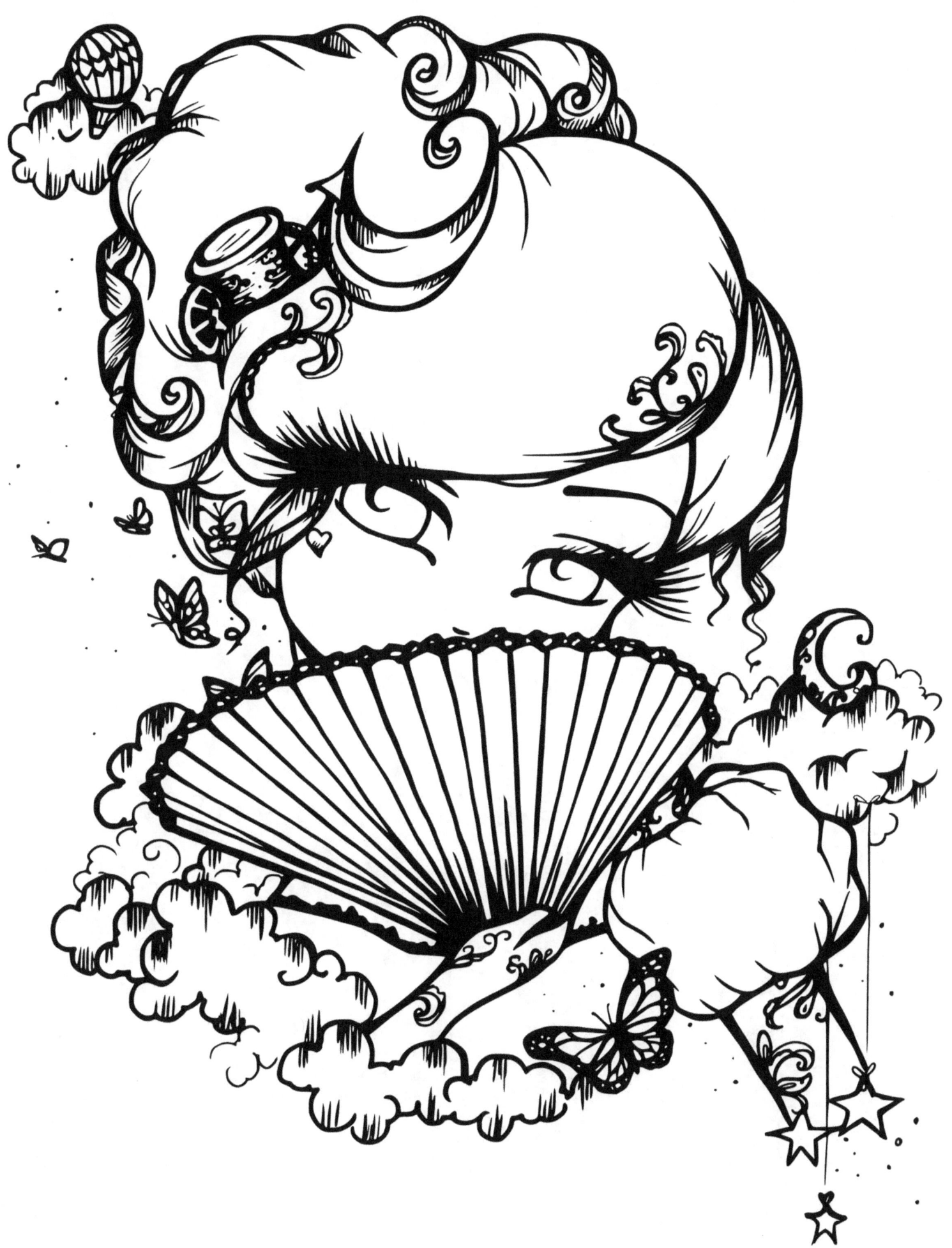

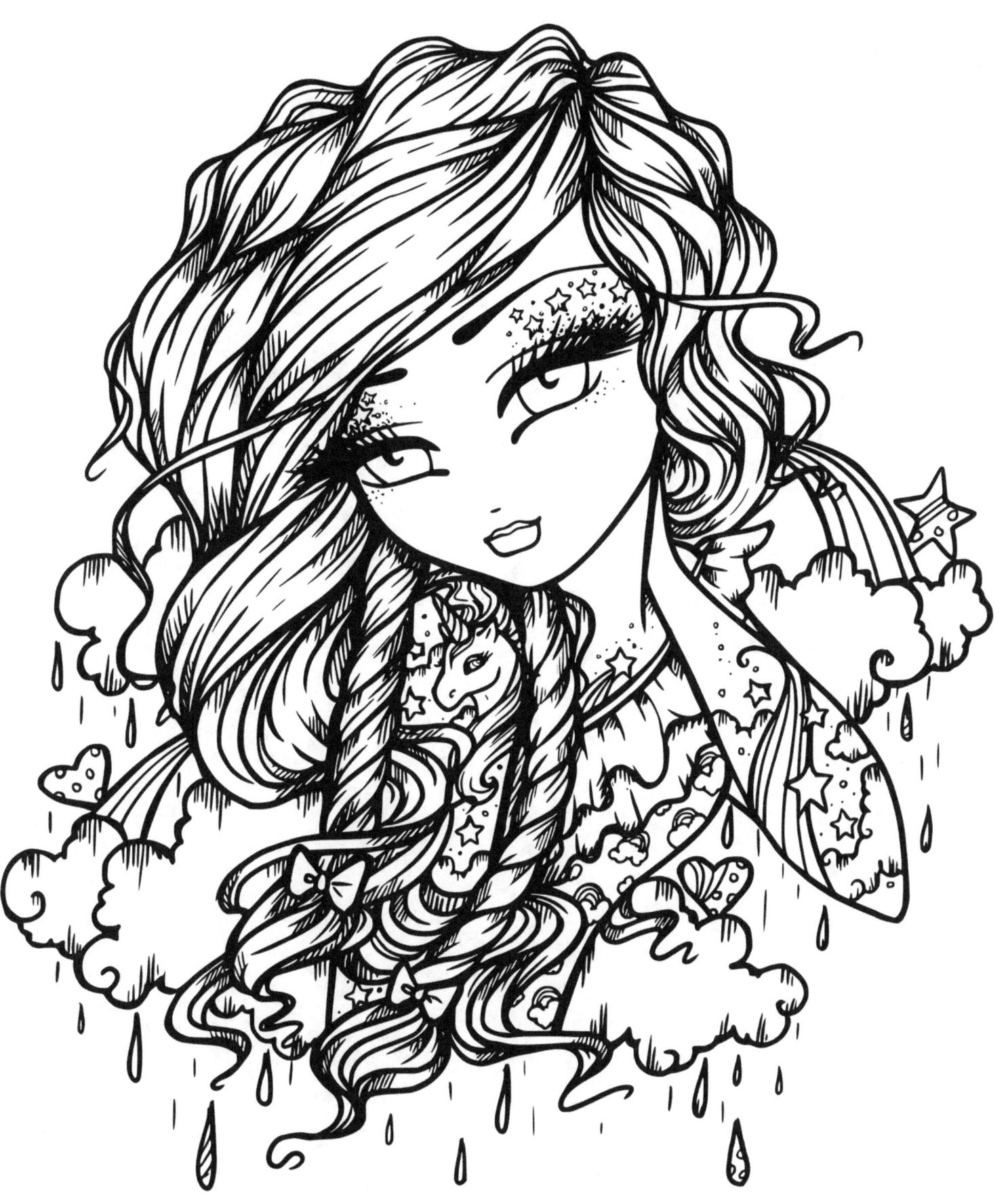

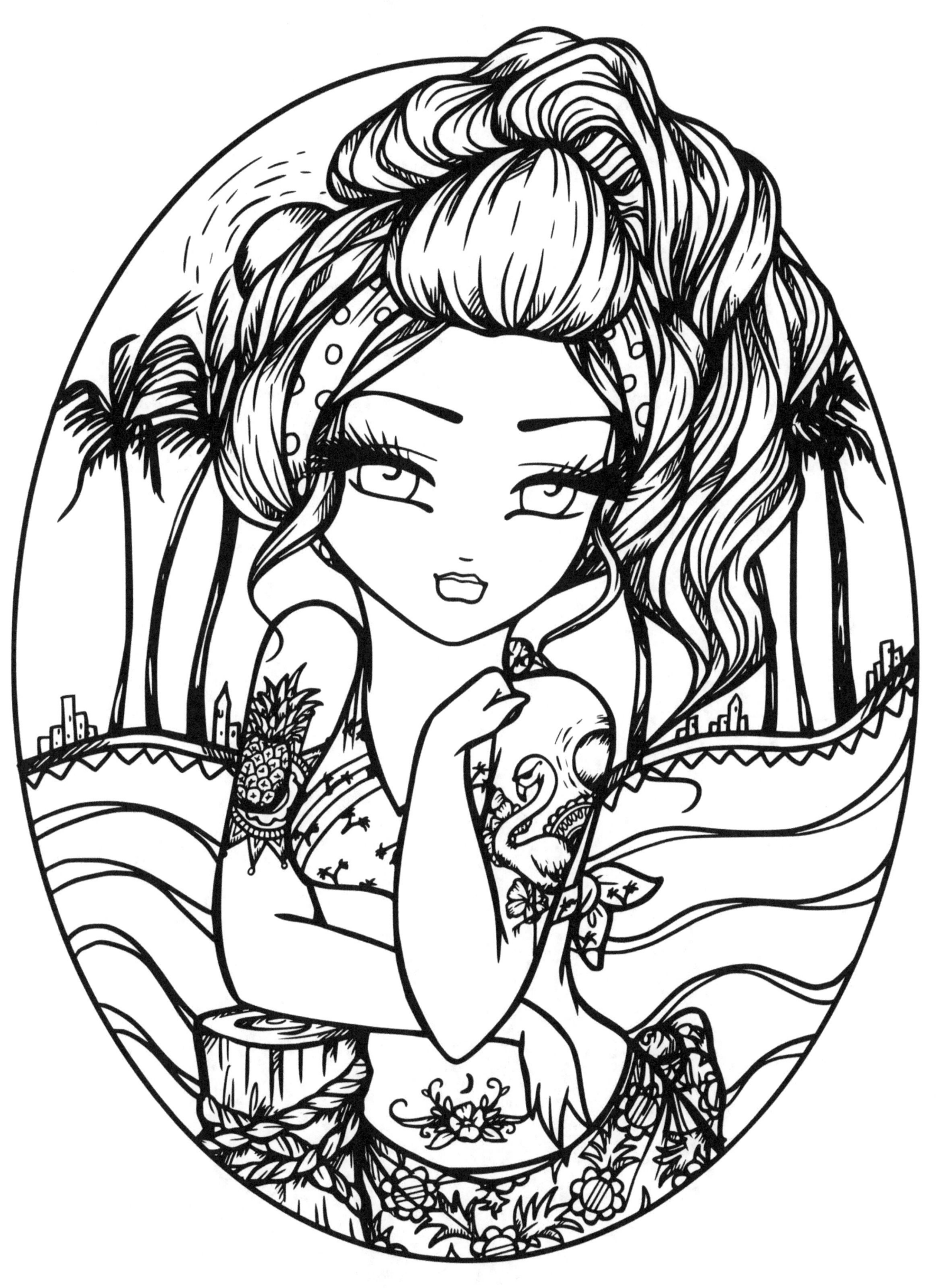

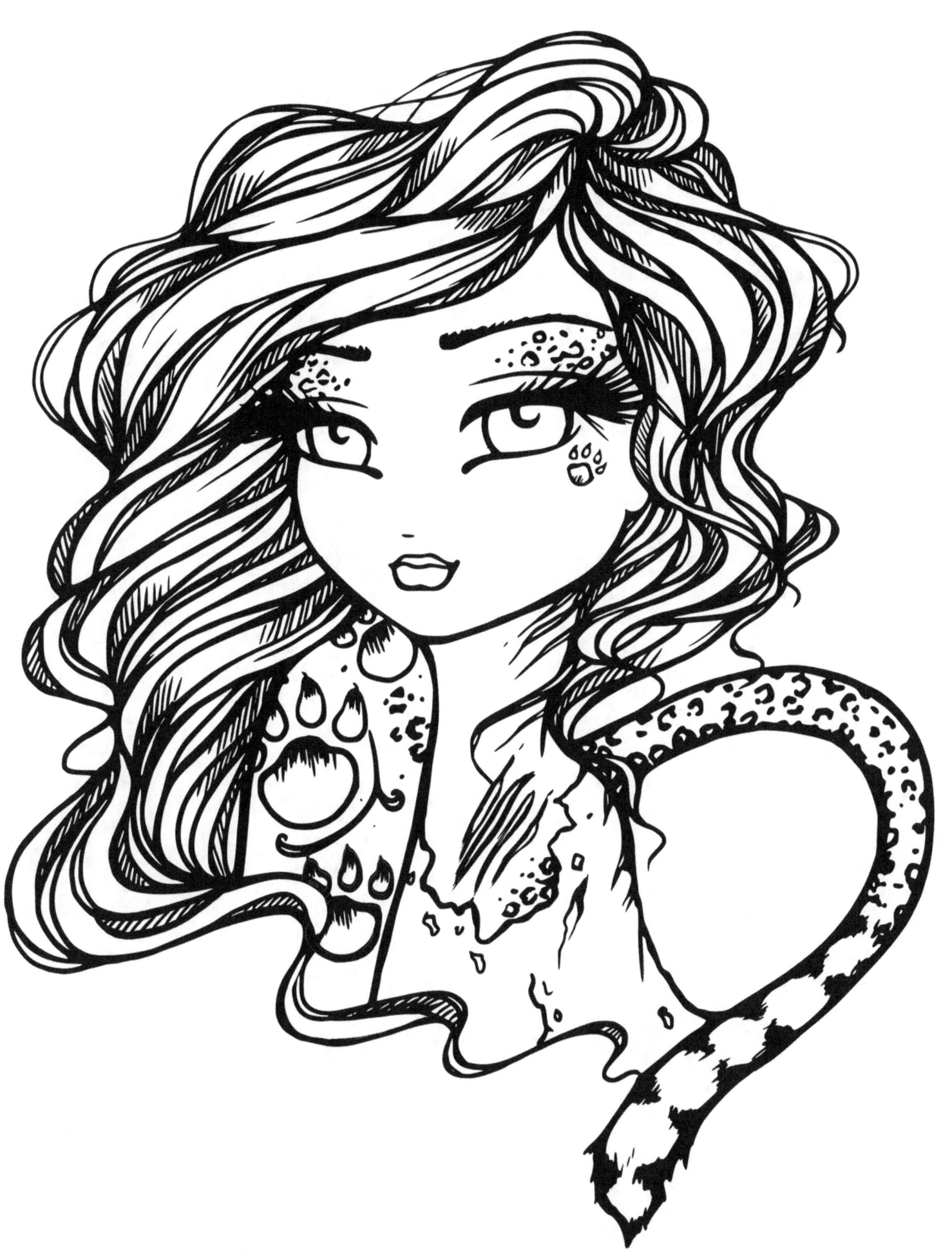

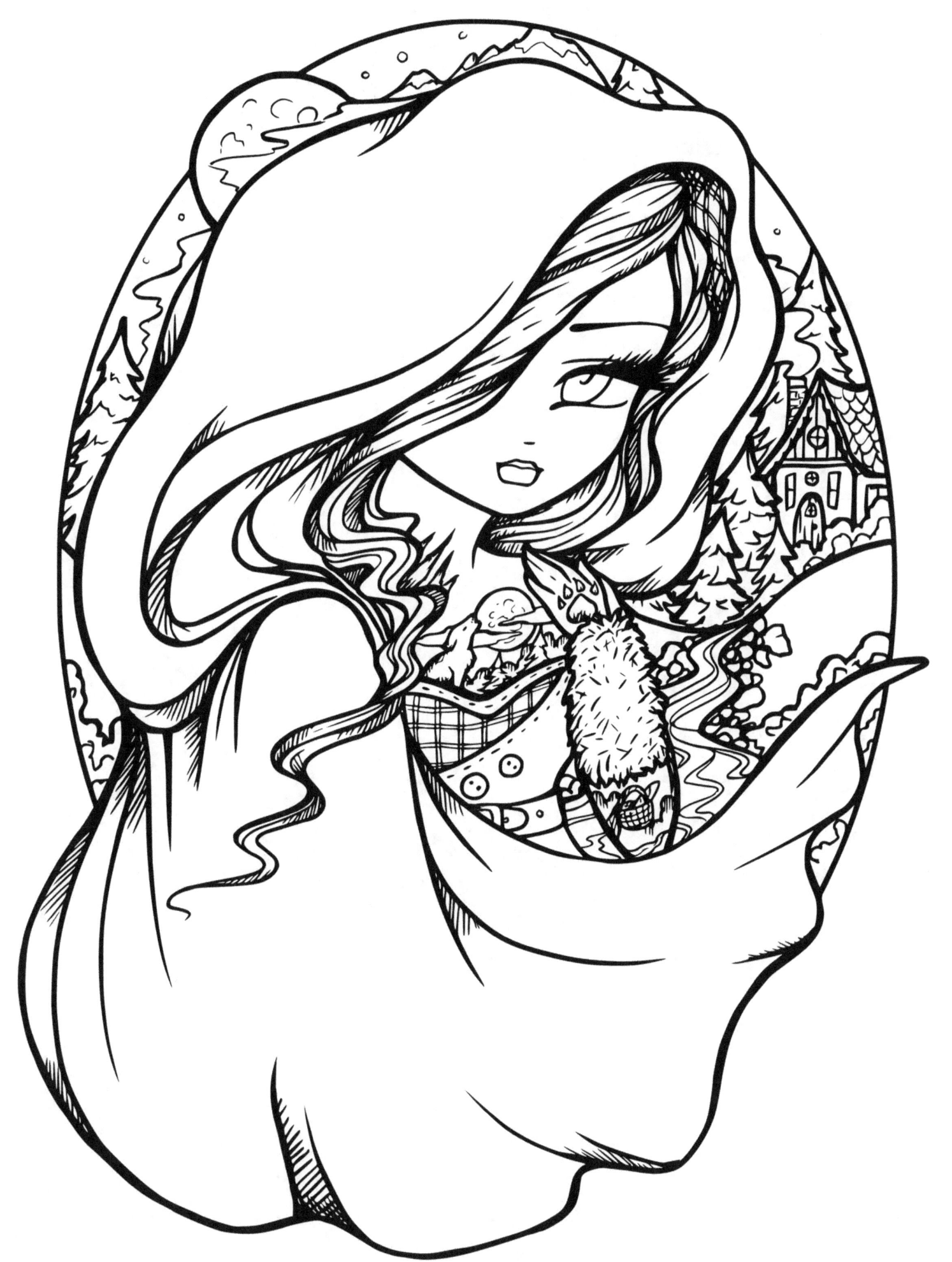

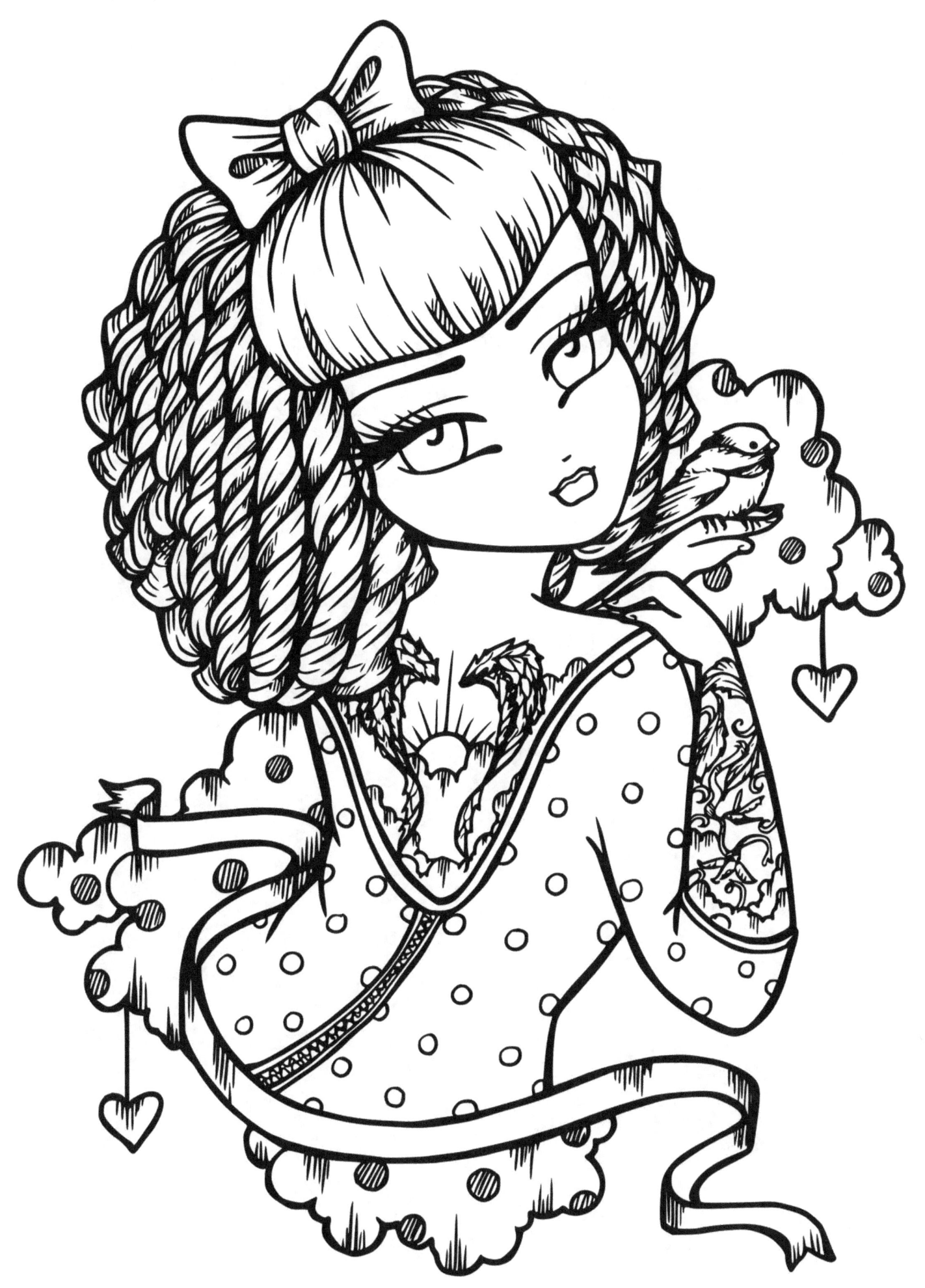

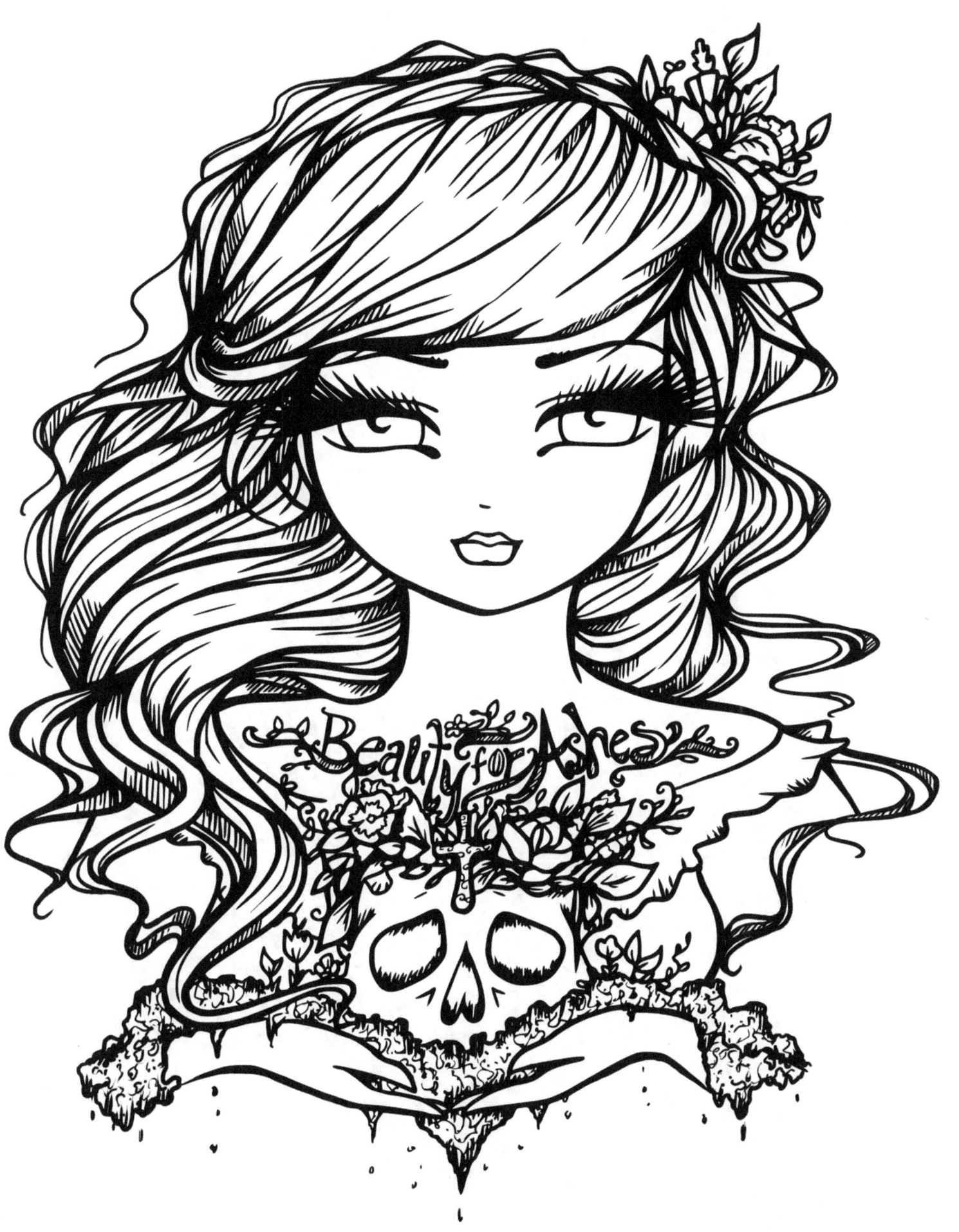

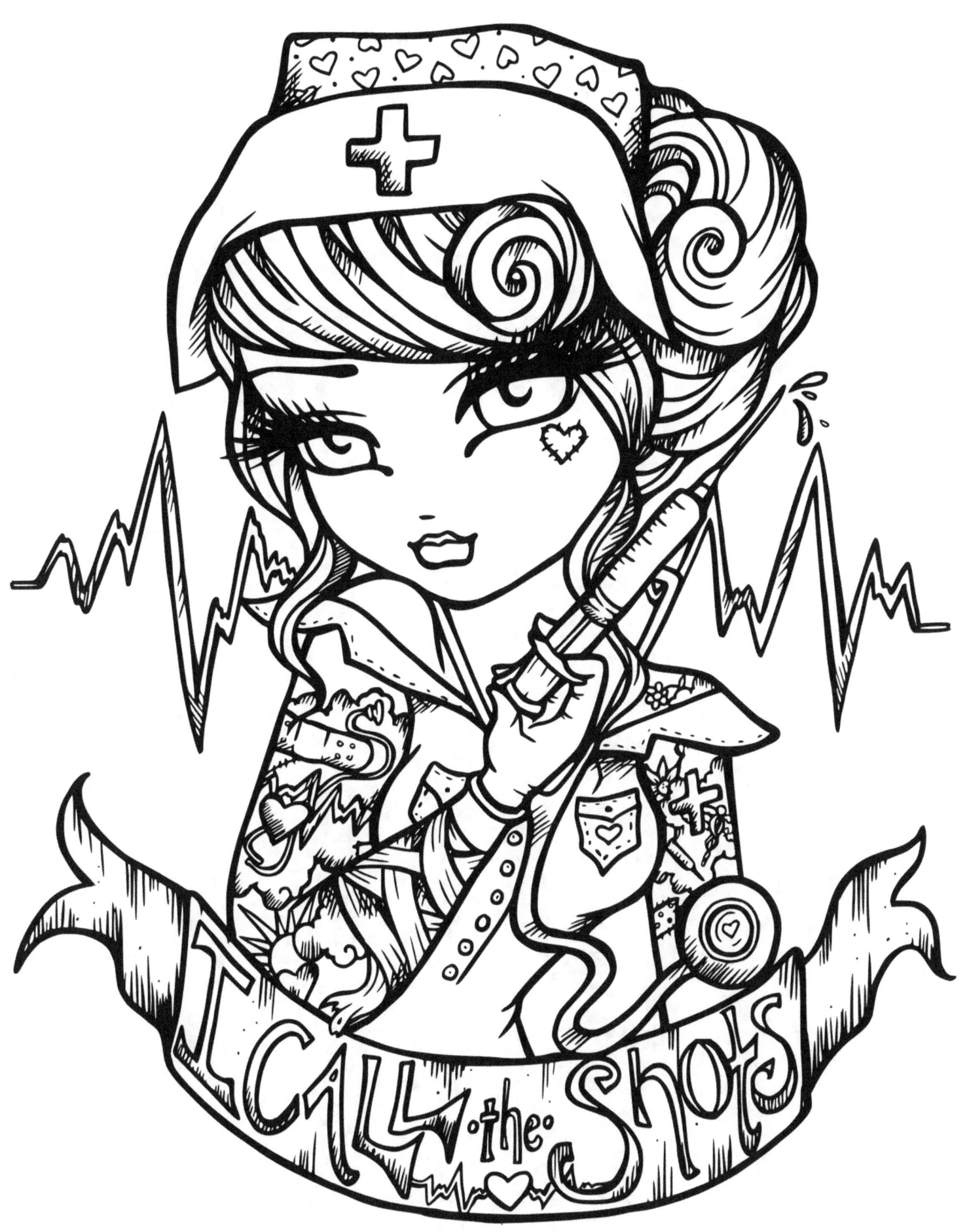

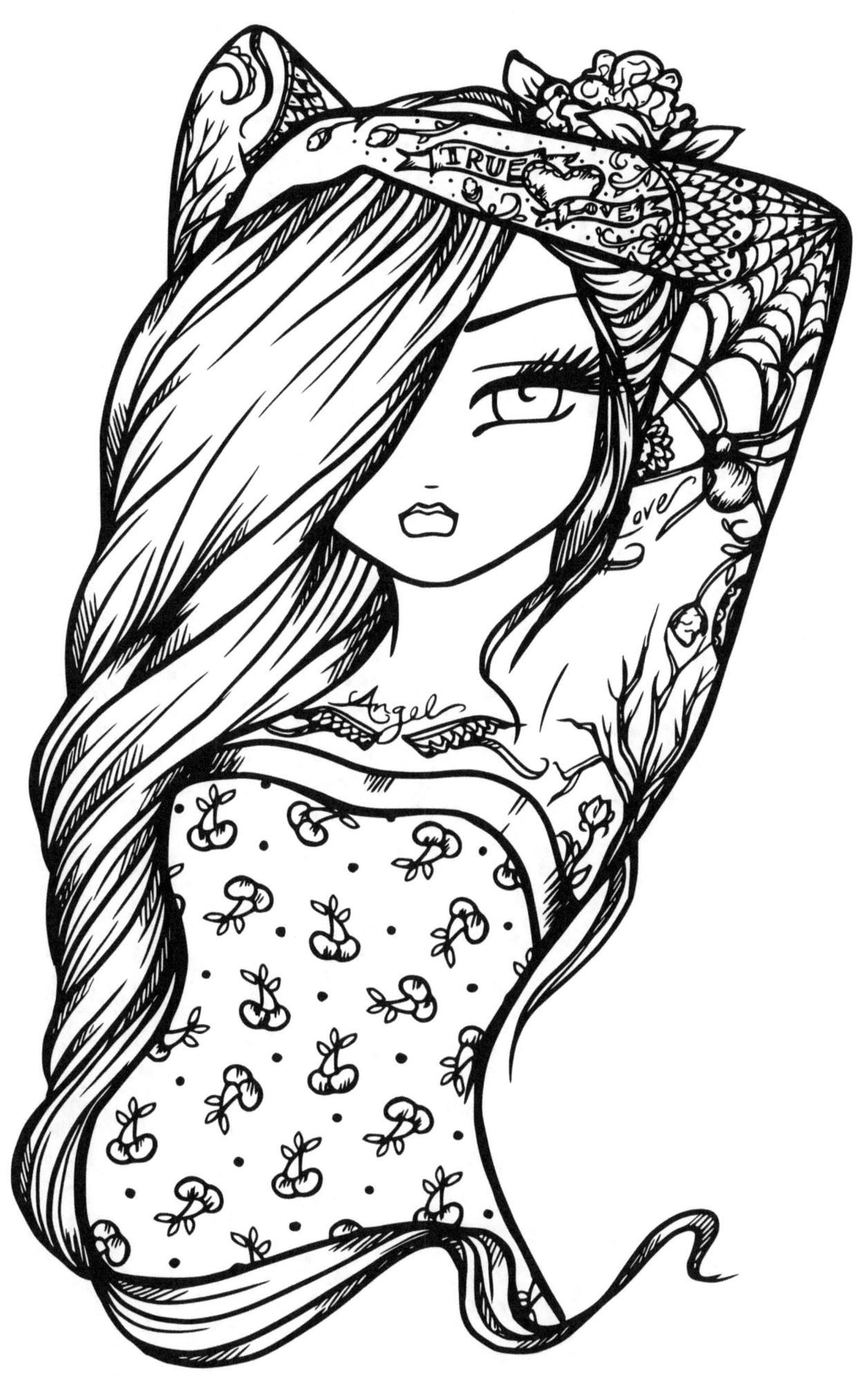

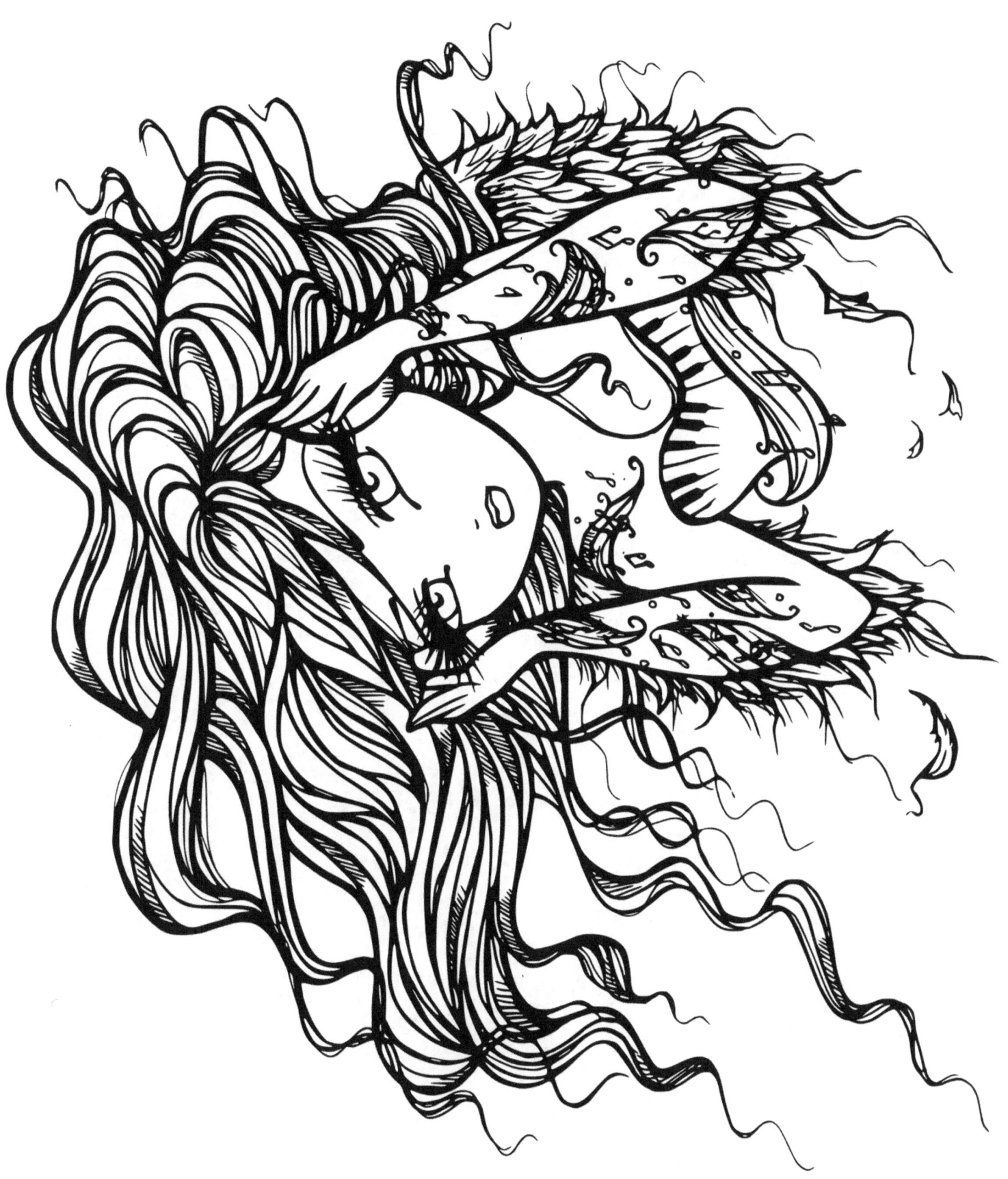

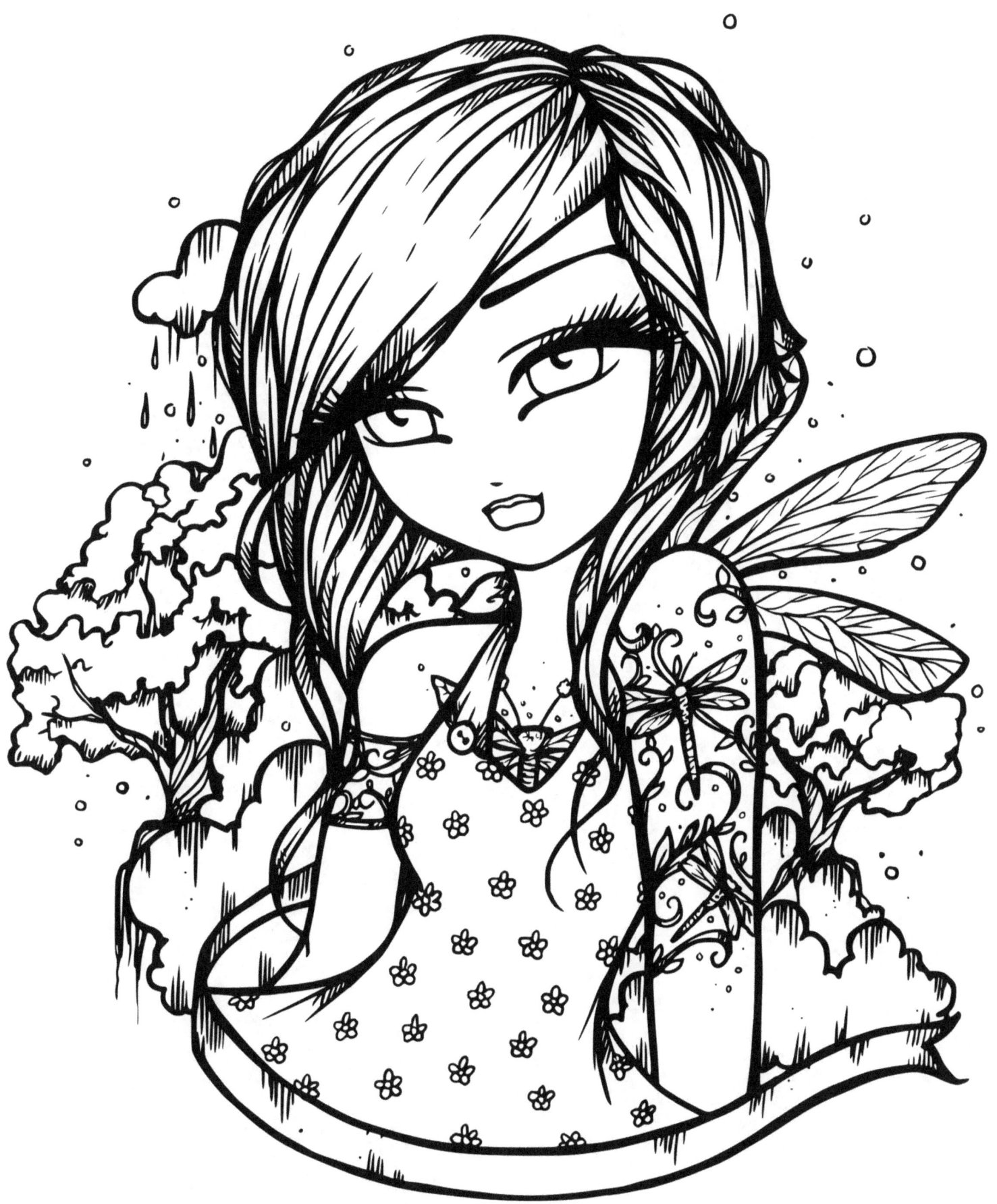

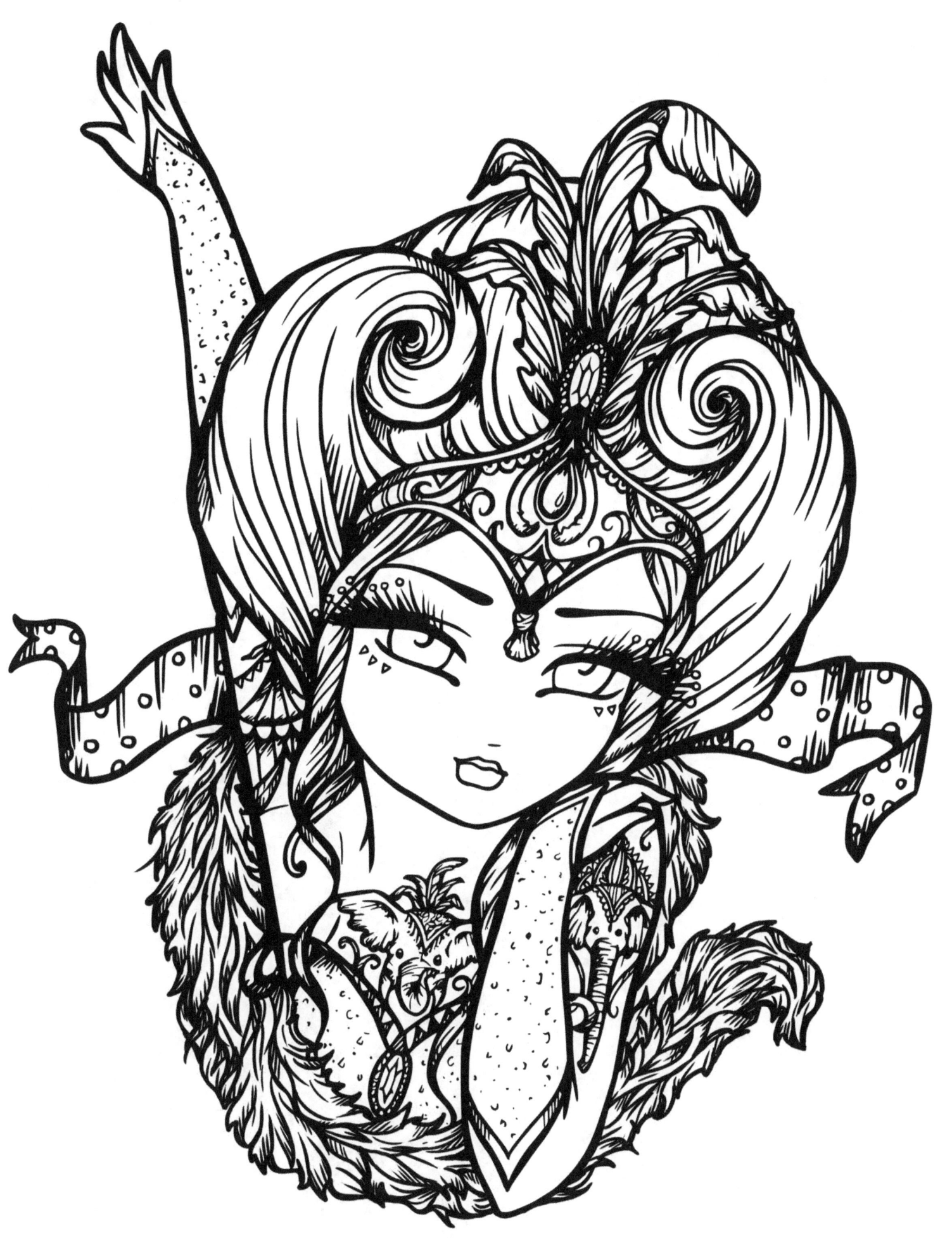

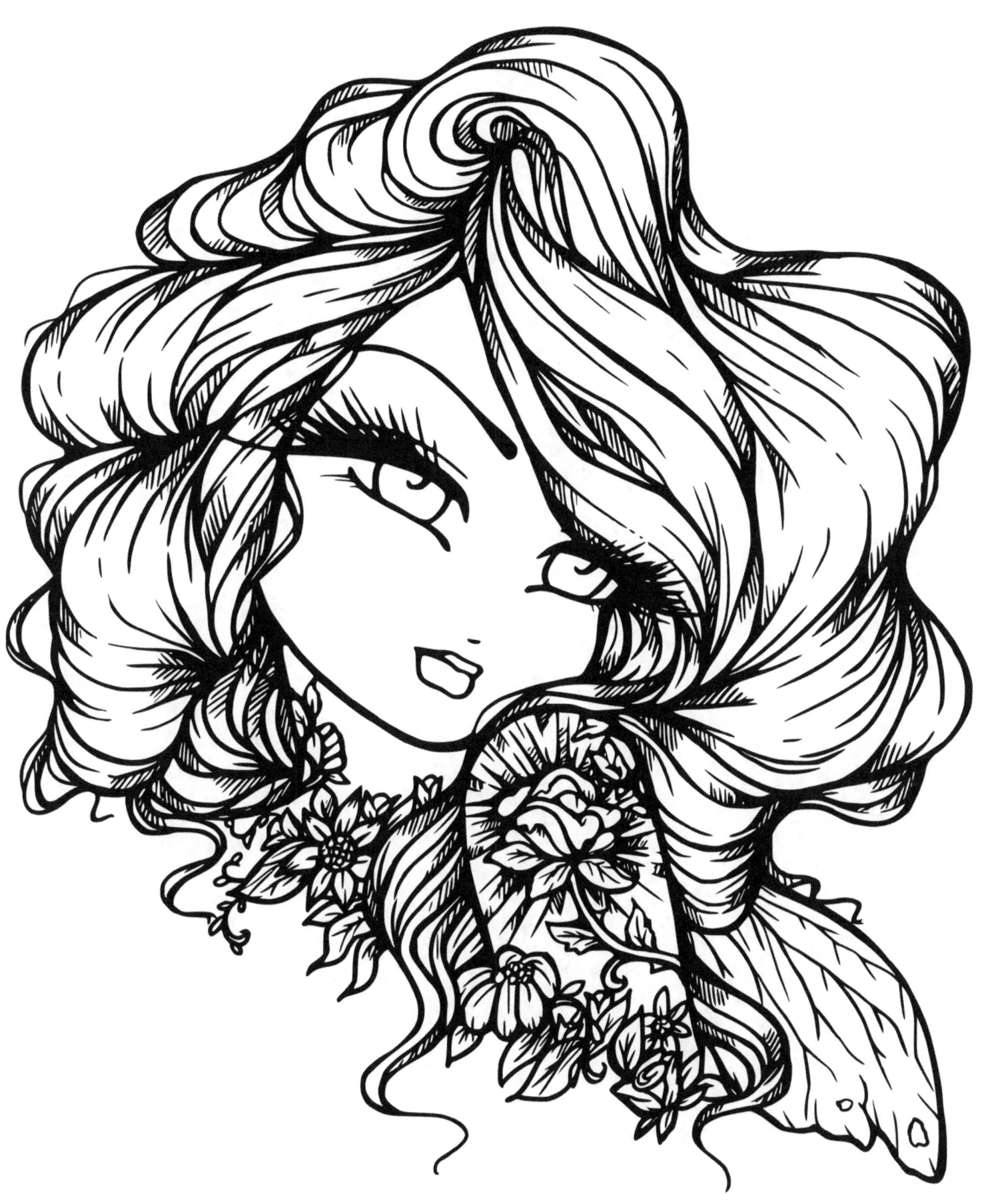

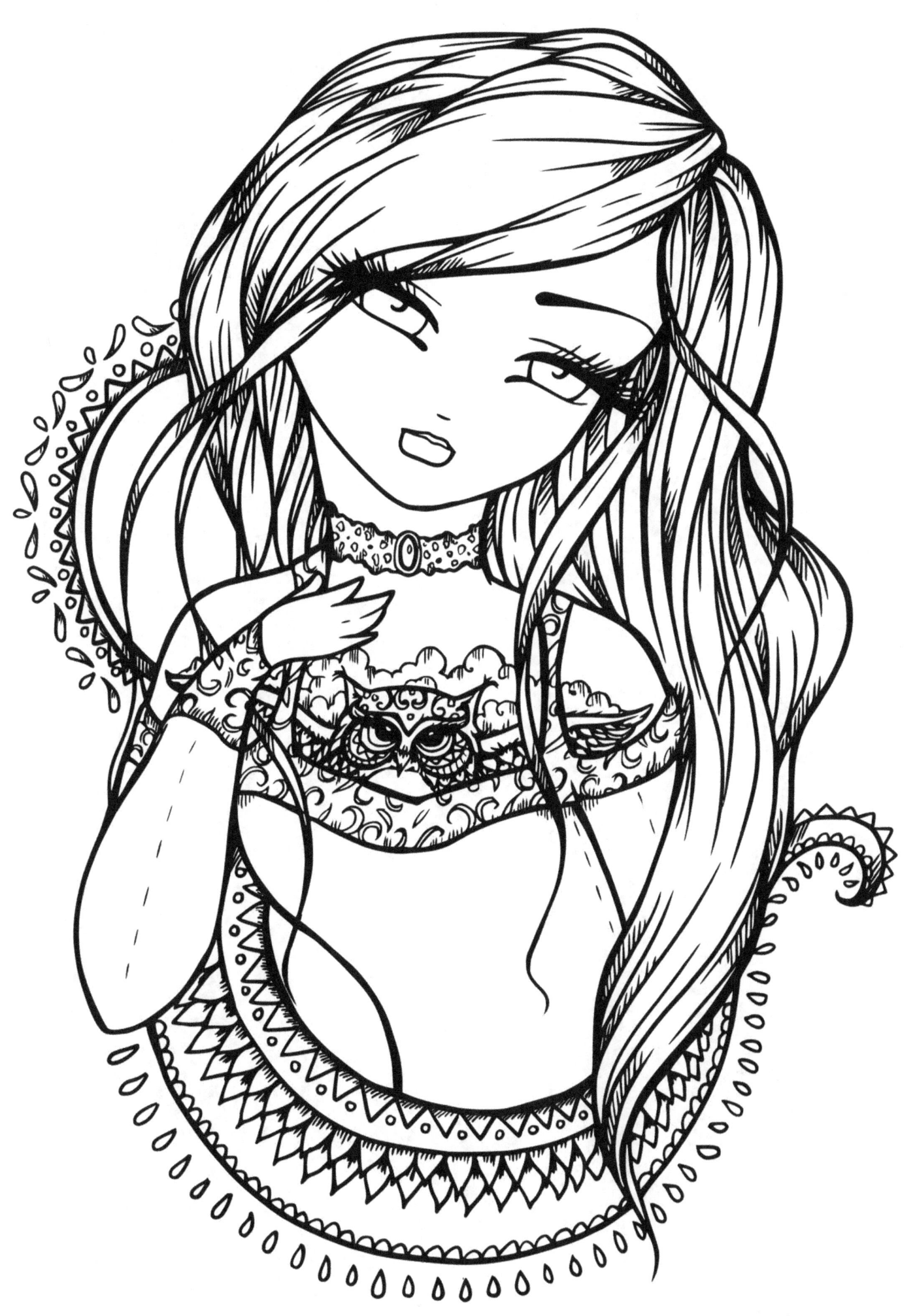

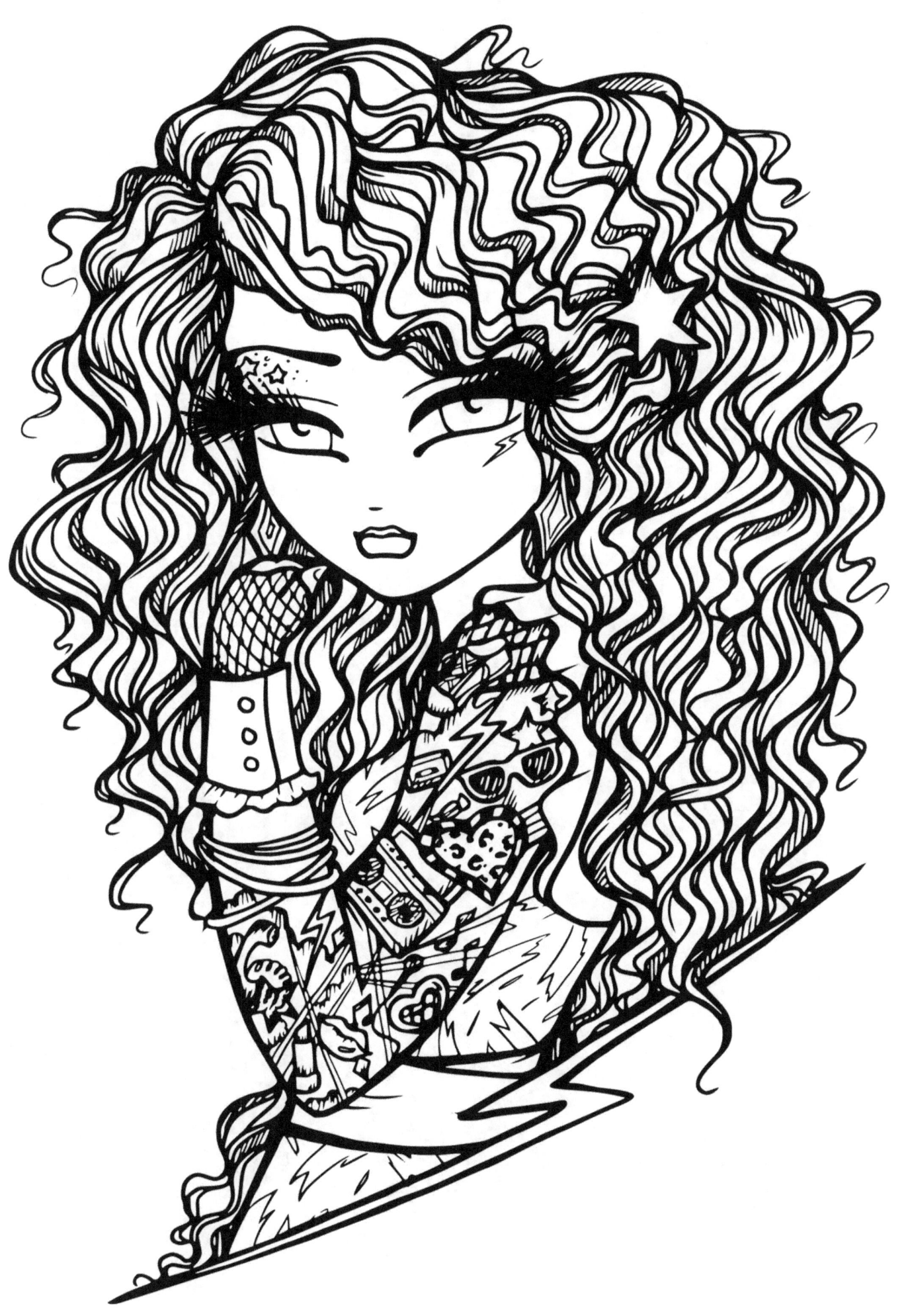

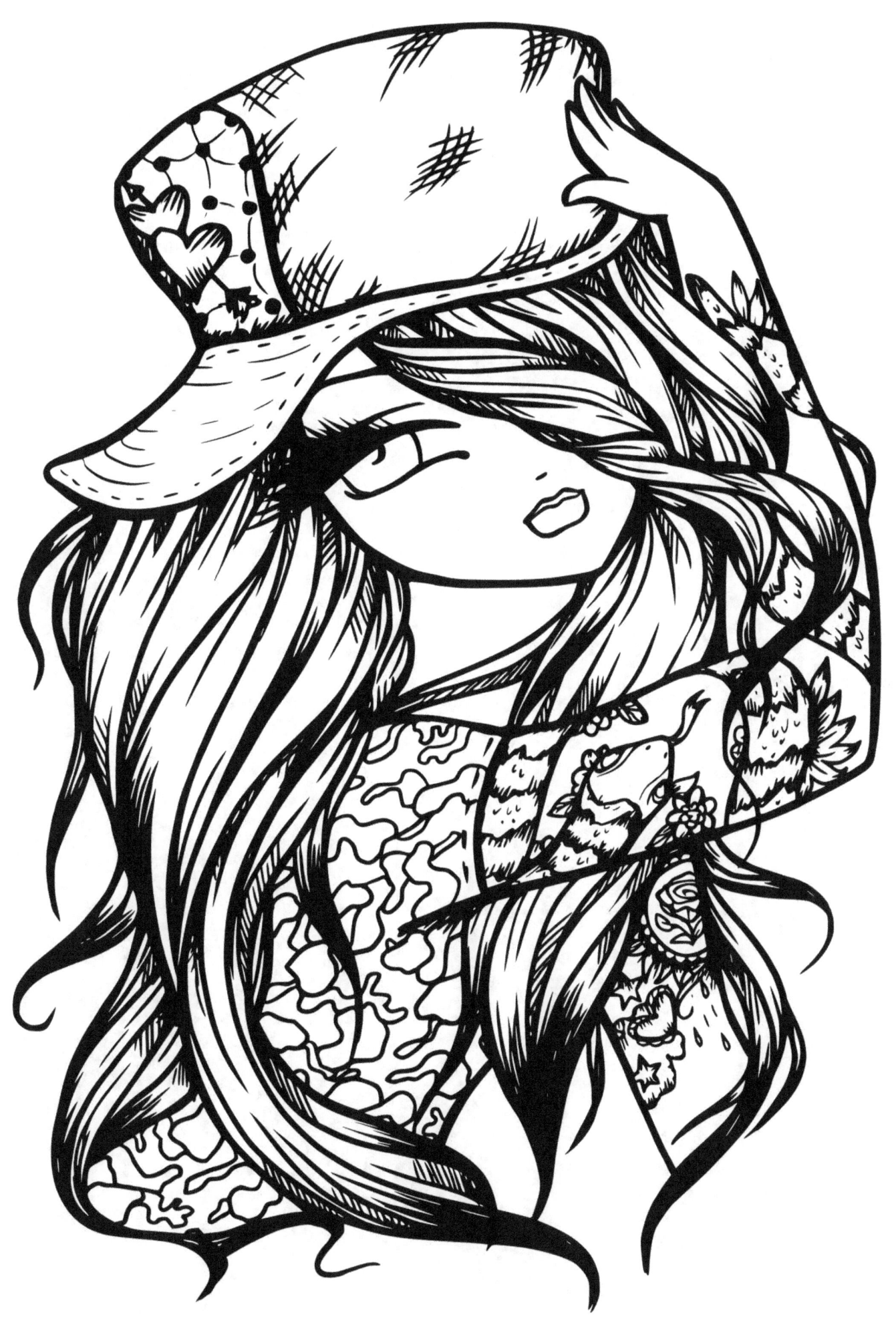

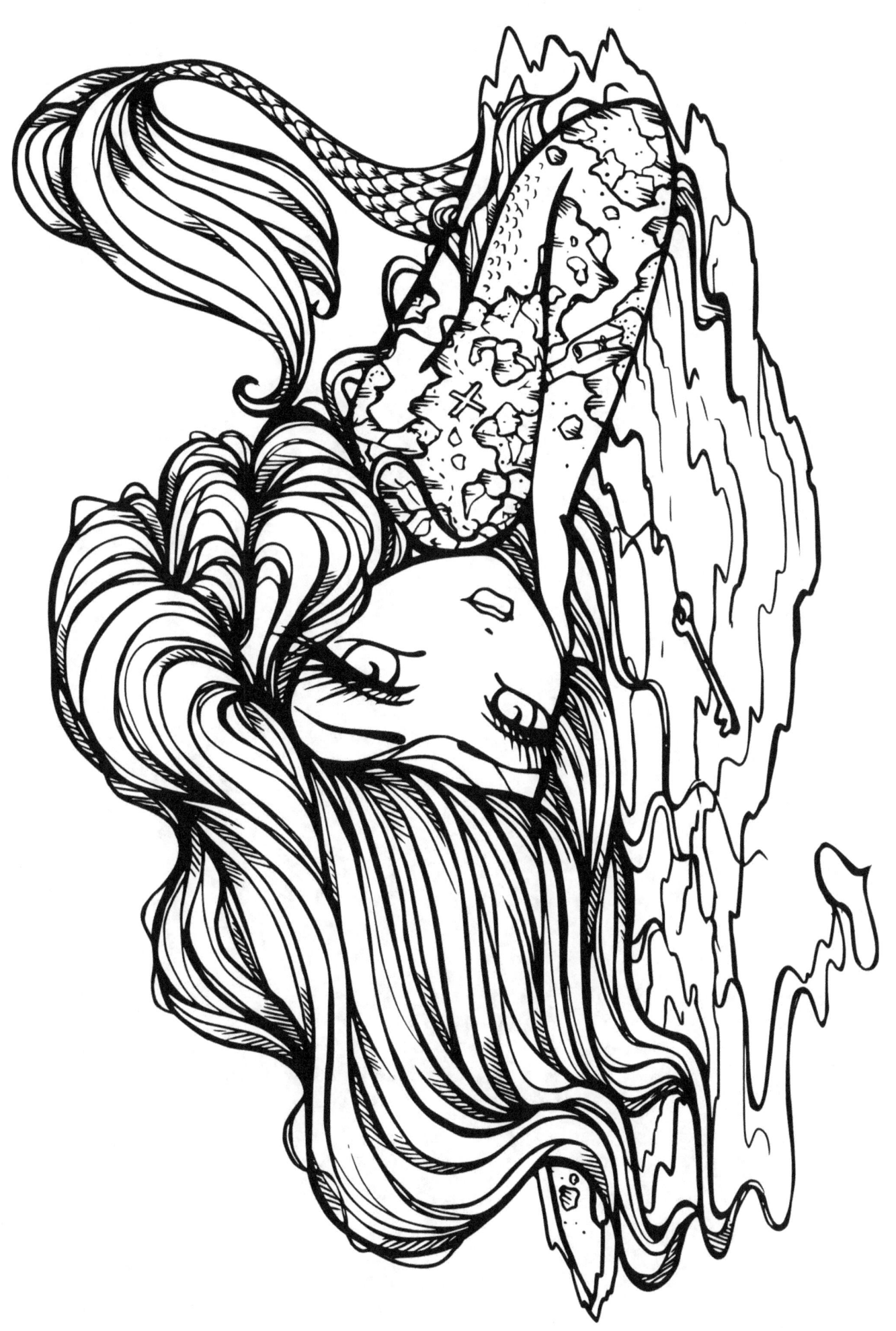

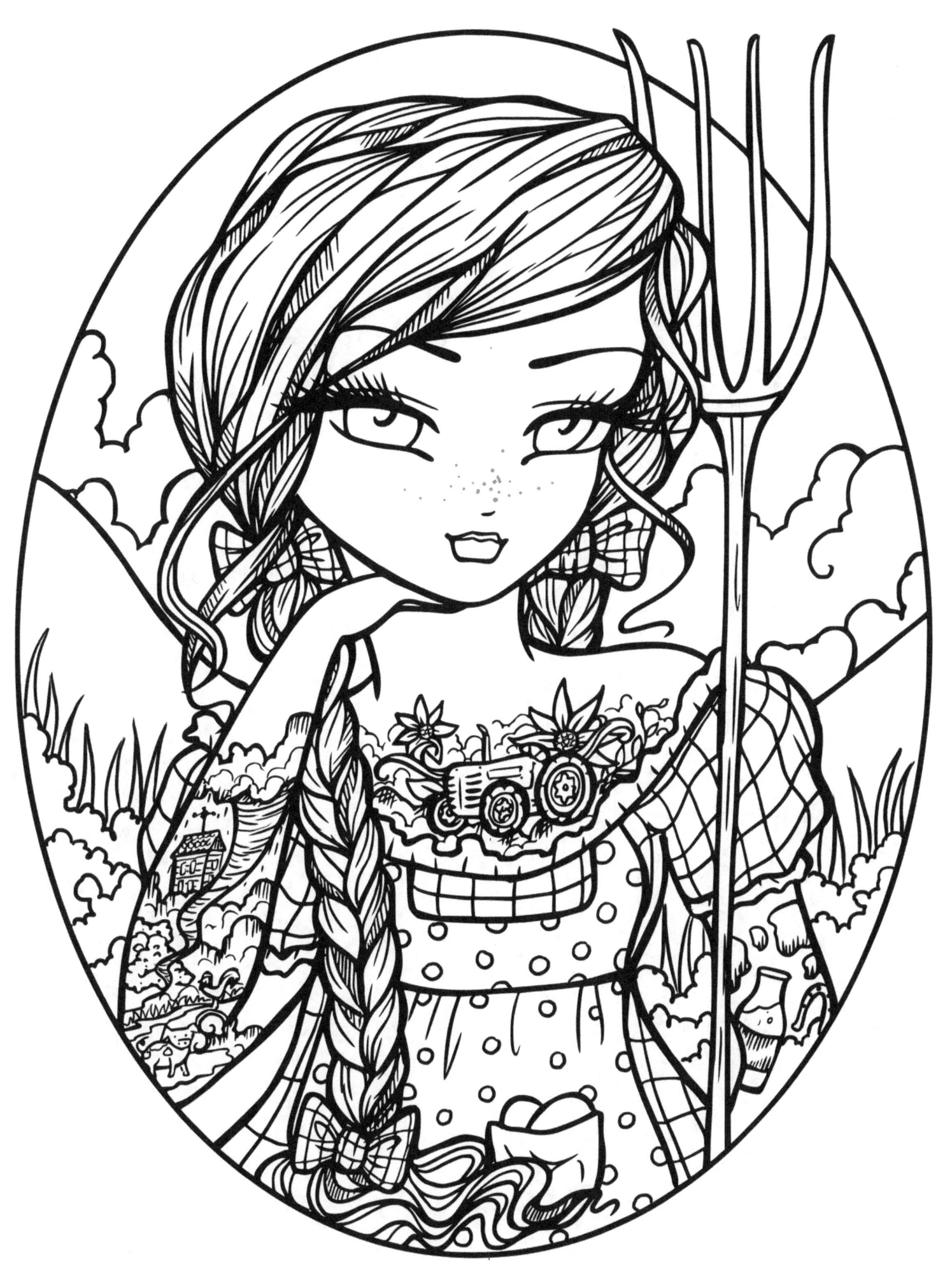

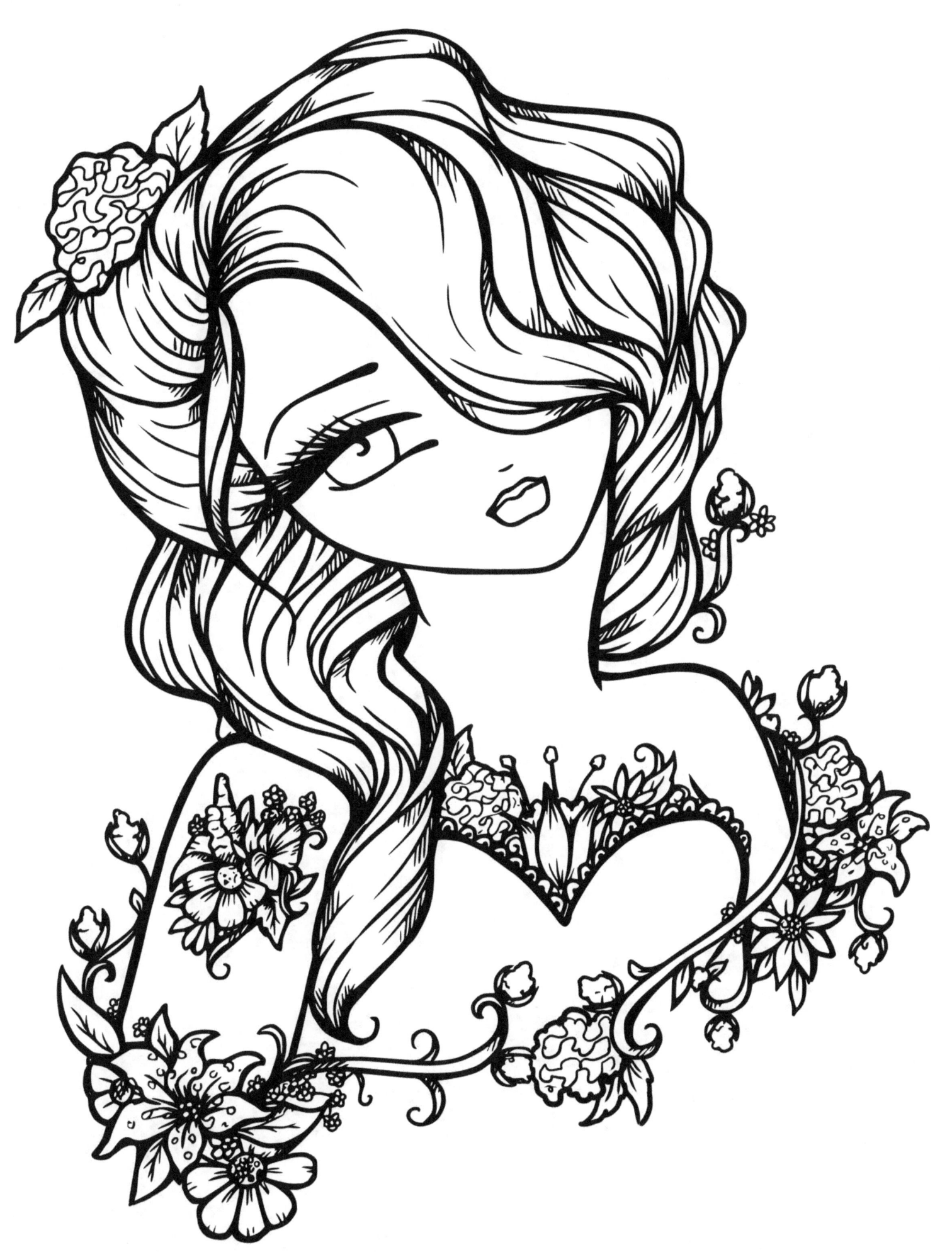

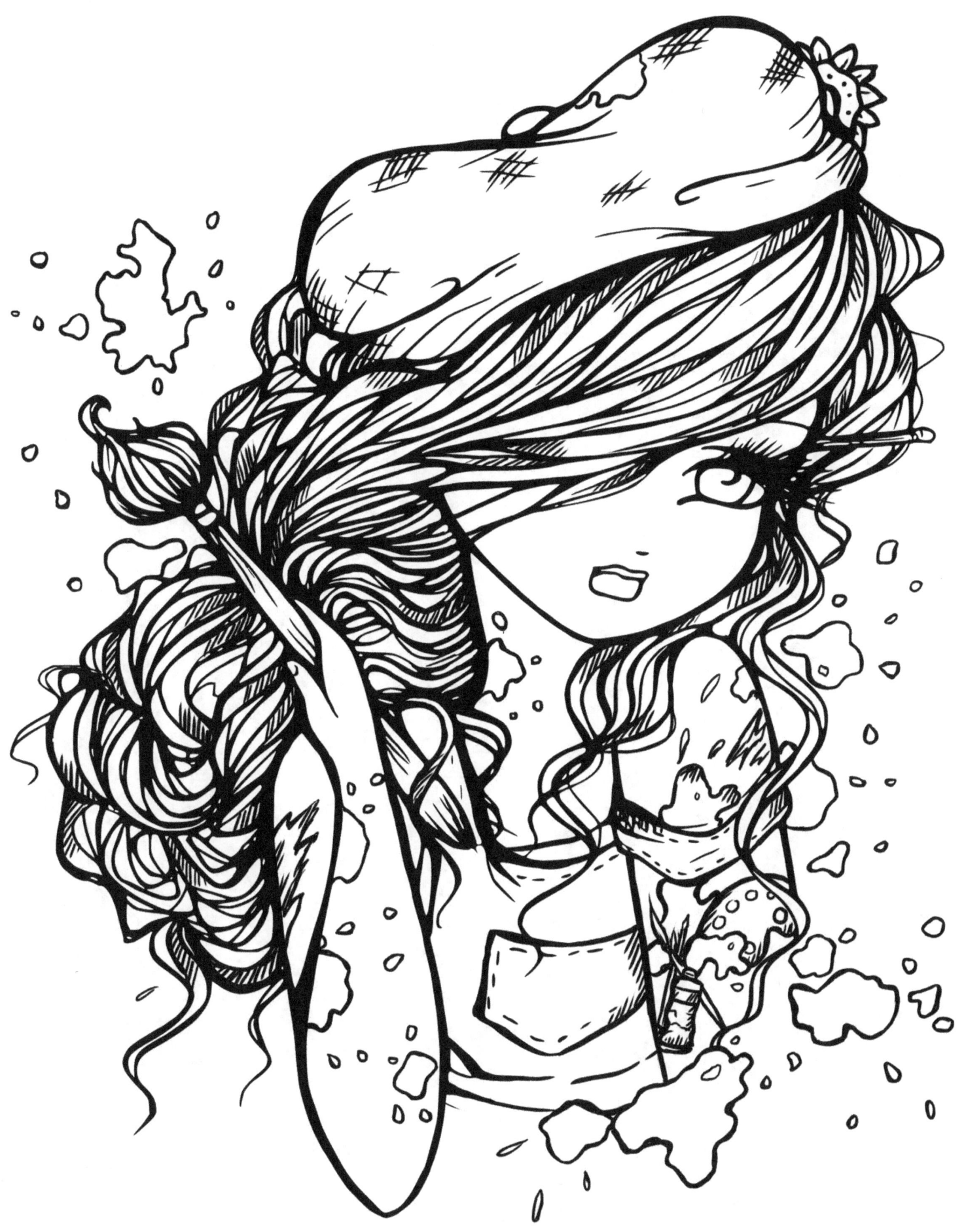

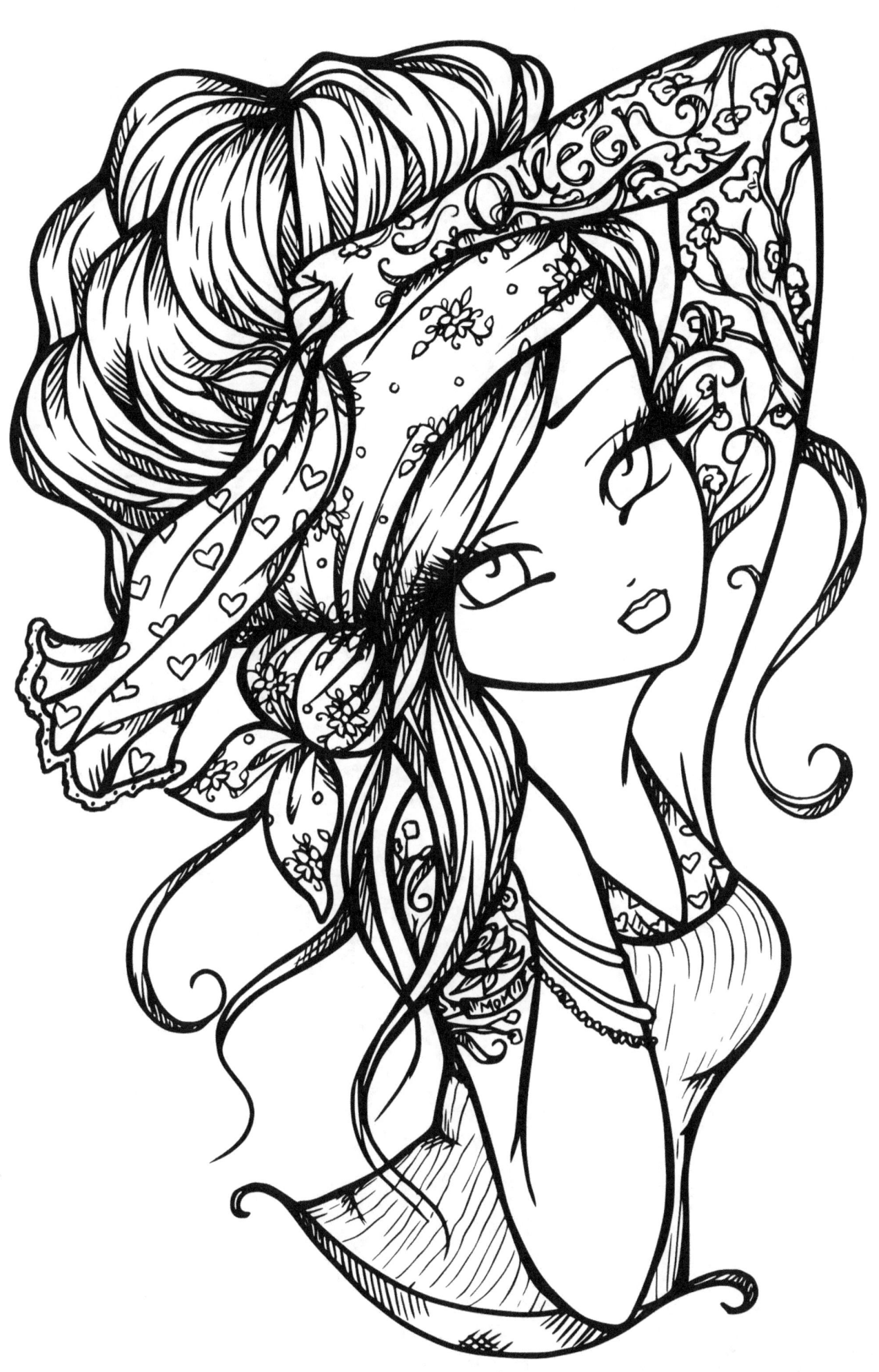

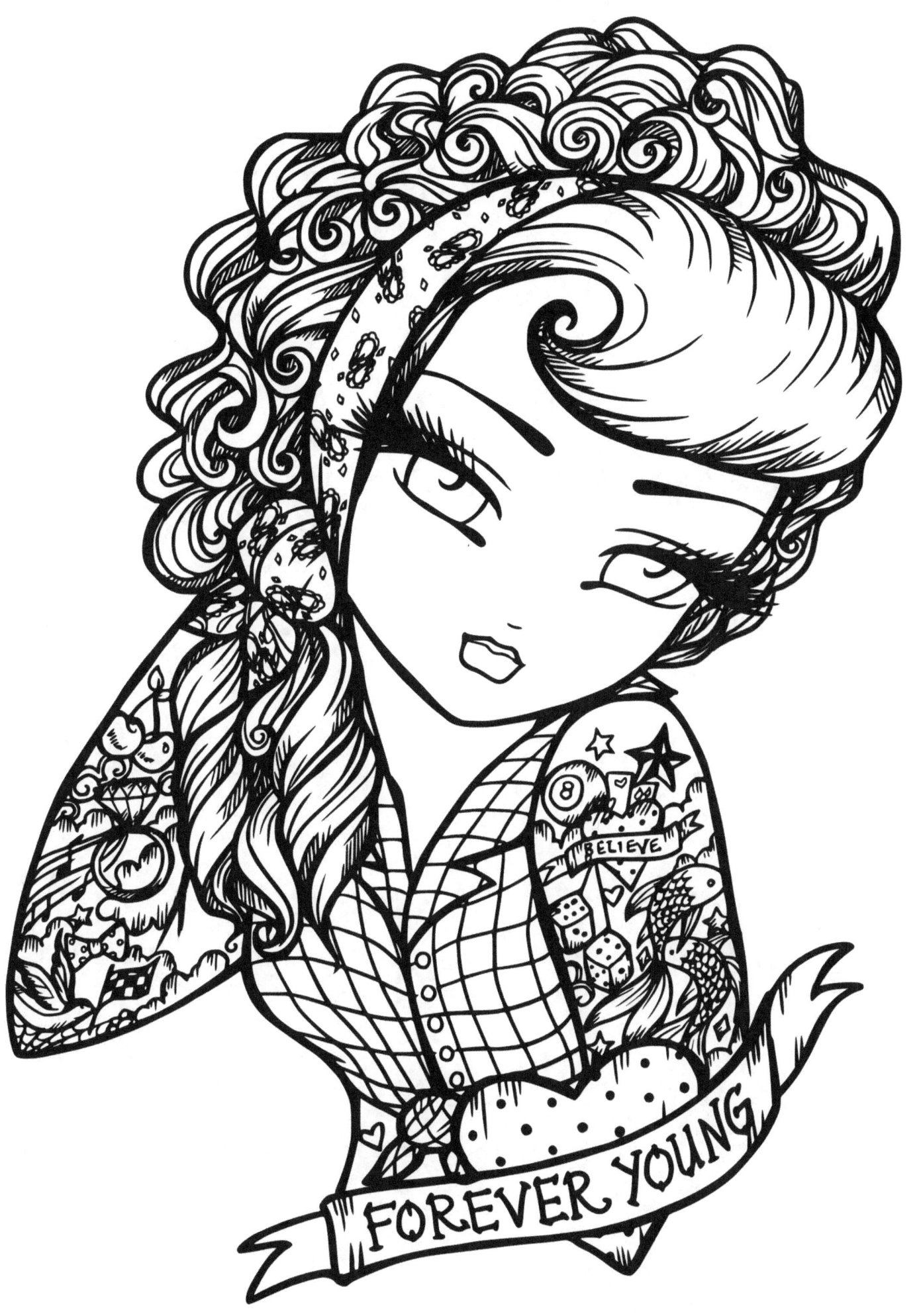

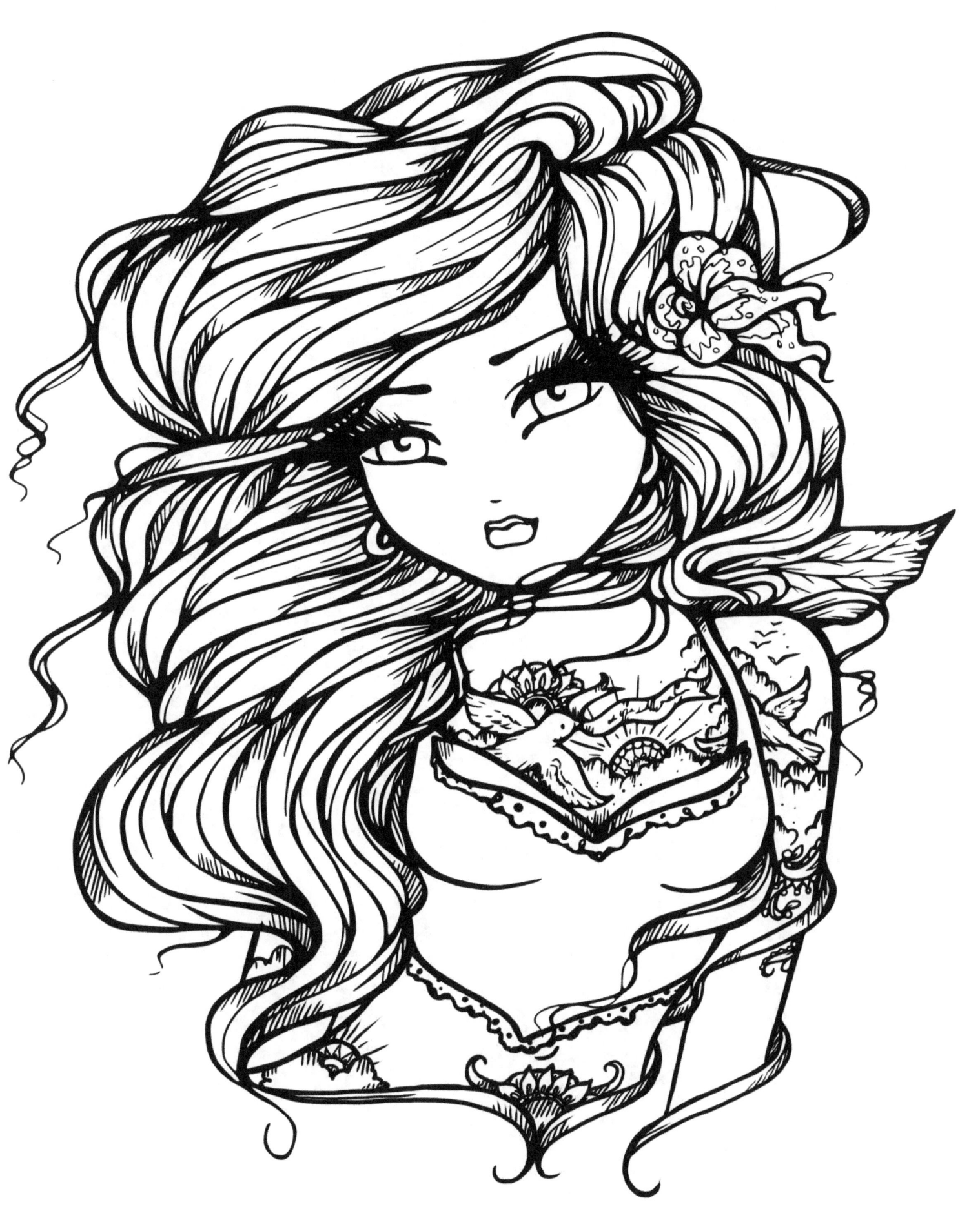

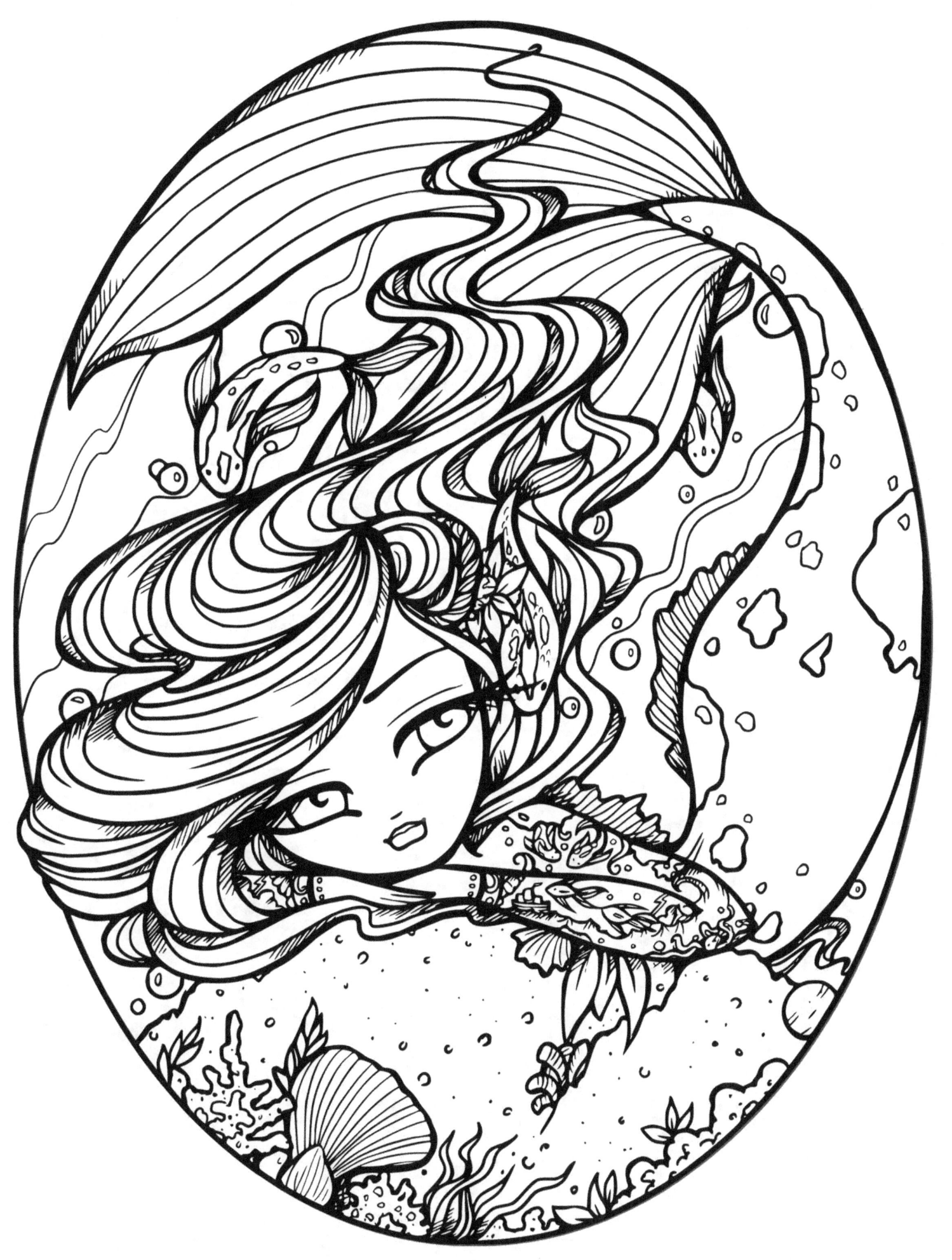

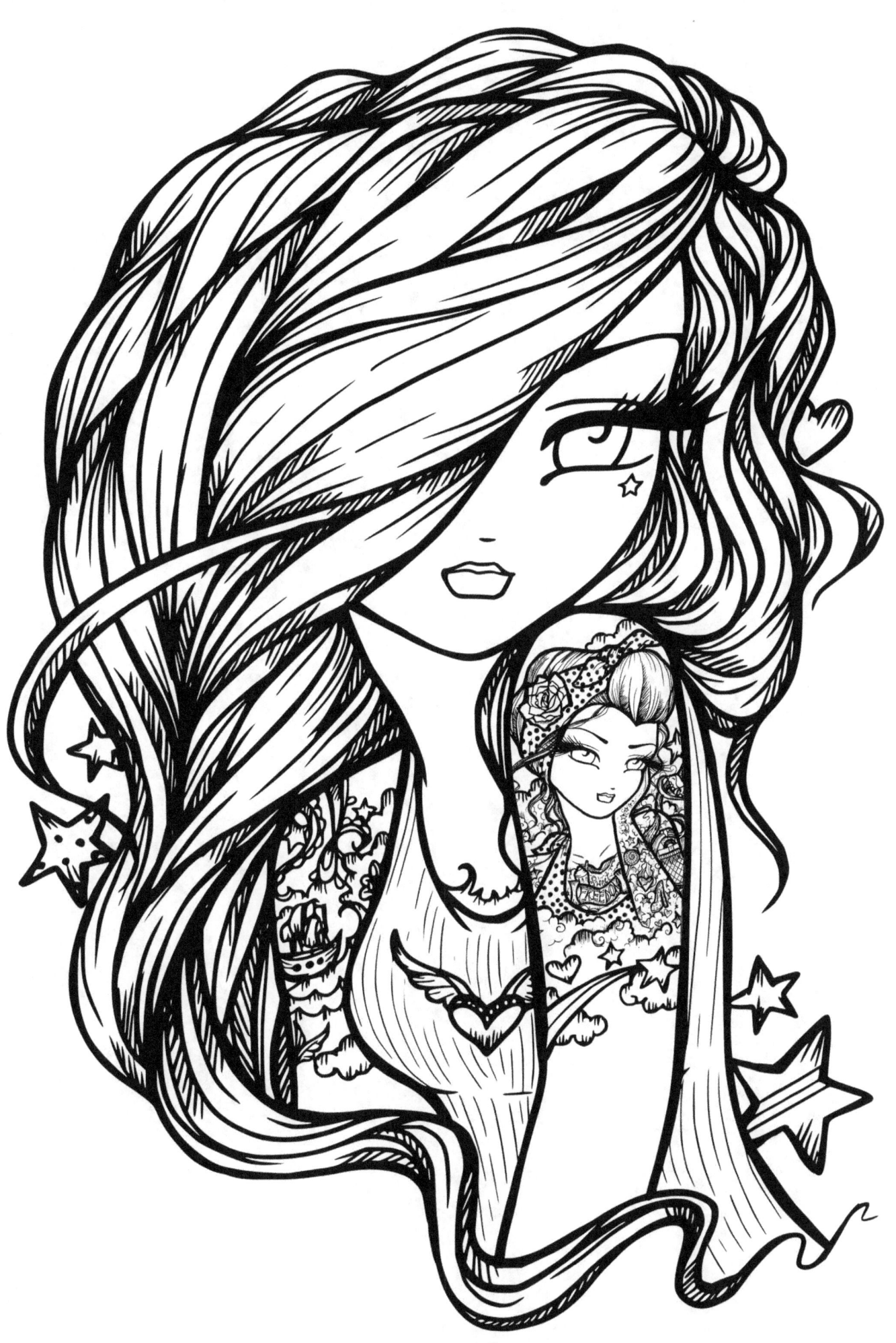